THE CONSEIL D'ETAT
IN MODERN FRANCE

NUMBER 603
COLUMBIA STUDIES IN THE SOCIAL SCIENCES
EDITED BY THE FACULTY OF POLITICAL
SCIENCE OF COLUMBIA UNIVERSITY

THE
CONSEIL D'ETAT
IN MODERN FRANCE

CHARLES E. FREEDEMAN

AMS PRESS
NEW YORK

COLUMBIA UNIVERSITY
STUDIES IN THE
SOCIAL SCIENCES

603

The Series was formerly known as
Studies in History, Economics and Public Law.

Reprinted with the permission of Columbia University Press
From the edition of 1961, New York
First AMS EDITION published 1968
Manufactured in the United States of America

Library of Congress Catalogue Card Number: 68-59255

AMS PRESS, INC.
NEW YORK, N. Y. 10003

TO MY PARENTS

PREFACE

THIS study is concerned with a period of history when France's governmental institutions were transformed by the development of democracy. The change in French governmental institutions was analogous to that which took place in other Western democracies. While all Western countries adapted their governmental institutions to changing conditions, each tried to meet the problem in its own way. The subject of this study affords an example of one of the contrasting ways in which the problem was met.

The Conseil d'Etat is particularly related to two of the most striking developments of this period. The first development is the great increase in legislation and in executive regulations, reflecting a growth in the functions of the state and making necessary the growth of bureaucracy. As a result the contacts between the individual and the state have multiplied, inevitably giving rise to conflicts between the two. The second development concerns the settlement of these conflicts between the individual and the state, which has become a problem in all Western democracies and has a direct bearing on the degree and scope of civil liberties. The Conseil d'Etat is an institution which has been at the center of these two developments. Therefore the Conseil's role in the formulation of the increasing volume of legislation and executive regulations, as well as its role as a court which adjudicates conflicts between the individual and the state, is of great significance. The French experience with these problems is instructive when compared with the method of handling these problems in other Western countries, and is essential for understanding the working of contemporary French governmental institutions.

The purpose of this study is to furnish a picture of the development and working of this institution and to inquire into the nature and scope of the transformations it has undergone. Since institutions are not organic entities having an independent existence of their own, but are made up of men, who contribute their effort, furnish guidance, and largely determine its destiny, some attention to these men, their background, recruitment, and training is necessary. For the period under consideration, from the fall of the Second Empire until the advent of the Fifth Republic, a number of individuals stand out as having affected the growth and development of the Conseil to a considerable degree, but there is not, in Carlyle's sense, one or several "great" men who have shaped the Conseil. Rather, most of the developments have been the result of collective action in which the share of any individual cannot be delimited and, often, his identity is unknown.

All individuals in any period of history must act within the institutional framework in which they find themselves. Action is, and has been always, limited by the institutional framework of society. Likewise, activity within the Conseil has been limited by the Conseil's place within the network of French institutions and the organization of the Conseil itself. Therefore, in dealing with the Conseil d'Etat considerable attention has been given to its organization and modifications in its internal structure since 1872. The first three chapters of this study are devoted to the internal development of the Conseil.

Chapters 4 and 5 examine the Conseil d'Etat as technical counselor of the government. This role is not widely known. There is a tendency either to overlook the Conseil as technical counselor of the government or, going to the other extreme, to exaggerate greatly its powers in this sphere. Actually, its role has been considerable, but it does not "run the country."

PREFACE   ix

The last two chapters deal with the Conseil as the highest administrative court. It is here that the greatest originality of the Conseil lies. It has long attracted attention from Anglo-American legal scholars from the time of A. V. Dicey's *Introduction to the Study of the Law of the Constitution*, which first appeared in 1885. At first they found more to blame than to praise, but with greater familiarity and advances in the jurisprudence of the Conseil in the last seventy years, the attitude has changed to one of general admiration.

A problem arising in this study was whether or not to translate French terms. I have attempted to give American equivalents for most French legal terms. In many instances the reader familiar with French may not be happy with my choice, but I believed the convenience of an American equivalent for those who do not have a knowledge of French legal terminology outweighed the inconvenience of those who will see familiar terms in a strange form.

I wish to express my appreciation for permission to work in the library of the Conseil d'Etat at the Palais Royal in Paris and for the courtesy shown me there by the members of the Conseil and the librarians. I am indebted to M. Henry Puget, Conseiller d'Etat, for answering many of my questions. M. Pierre Laroque, Conseiller d'Etat, Dr. Frederic S. Burin, Professor Jacques Barzun, and Professor Henry P. DeVries have read the entire manuscript in various stages of its development and have offered much valuable criticism. Elizabeth M. Evanson of Columbia University Press has given me editorial assistance. Most of all I am indebted to Professor Shepard B. Clough, who first stimulated my interest in the Conseil and guided my research and writing through every stage. Each of these individuals contributed to making this a better book and have kept me from many errors. Their advice was not followed in all matters and whatever deficiencies the book has are my own responsibility.

Stevens Point, Wisconsin   C.E.F.
September, 1960

CONTENTS

1. The Place of the Conseil d'Etat among French Institutions — 1
2. The Structure of the Conseil d'Etat, 1872–1940 — 15
3. The Structure of the Conseil d'Etat since 1940 — 45
4. The Legislative Function of the Conseil d'Etat since 1872 — 72
5. The Administrative Function of the Conseil d'Etat since 1872 — 92
6. The Judicial Function of the Conseil d'Etat since 1872: I — 111
7. The Judicial Function of the Conseil d'Etat since 1872: II — 140

Appendix A. Opinion of the Conseil d'Etat of February 6, 1953, Concerning Article 13 of the Constitution — 169

Appendix B. Number of Cases Decided by the Conseil d'Etat, 1852–1958 — 171

Notes — 173
Bibliography — 195
Table of Cases — 199
Index — 201

THE CONSEIL D'ETAT
IN MODERN FRANCE

1

THE PLACE OF THE CONSEIL D'ETAT AMONG FRENCH INSTITUTIONS

IN recent years the French Conseil d'Etat has attracted the attention of an increasing number of Anglo-American scholars, as the growing literature on the subject attests. This interest has been generally confined to the judicial function of the Conseil in the field of administrative law, and is to be explained in part by the rapid growth during the last forty years of administrative law in Britain and the United States. Yet the Conseil d'Etat is also the technical counselor of the government and its activities in this capacity are worthy of investigation in an age of increasing government by the executive. This study will cover both roles that the Conseil has filled since the beginning of the Third Republic.

THE DUAL ROLE OF THE CONSEIL D'ETAT

From its early origins the Conseil d'Etat has played a double role in French public life. The modern Conseil d'Etat, created by the Constitution of the Year VIII (1799), had a large legislative and administrative role during the Consulate and a lesser one during the Empire. It formulated all the important legislation of the Consulate, such as the law reorganizing the administrative system which brought to fruition the process of centralization in France, the basic features of which are still retained. The *Code Civil* was drafted by a committee within the Conseil, with Bonaparte himself presiding over many of its meetings.

Since 1800 every one of the various political regimes has possessed a Conseil d'Etat. Actually, the concept of a Conseil was not original with the Consulate, as de Tocqueville has shown in his *L'Ancien régime et la Révolution*.[1] There is a considerable resemblance between the Conseil of the Consulate and the Conseil du Roi[2] of the *ancien régime*. Both performed functions roughly equivalent to the present functions of the Conseil as technical counselor and as administrative court. Both were reflections of a centralized administration. Both had different grades of members known as Councilors of State and Maîtres des Requêtes—titles which go back to the fourteenth century. However, in spite of these general resemblances, there are vast differences of degree between the functions and organization of the Conseil du Roi and the present Conseil d'Etat. Some of these differences are the result of changes in the form of government, some reflect changing economic and social conditions.

In the last fifty years the growth of social services performed by the state has greatly multiplied the points of contact between the citizen and his government, on the one hand, and has greatly increased the number and length of statutes, on the other. Consequently the staff and powers of ministerial departments have multiplied and the number of departments has almost doubled. The fitting of these developments into the framework of the nineteenth-century state has created many problems relative to the conservation of a democratic form of government and the protection of individual rights from undue infringement. In France the Conseil d'Etat has played an important part in these developments, and has in turn been altered to cope with them.

Because the legislative task has become so large and complicated, an ever increasing part of it has fallen to the executive, which supplements legislation by executive-made rules and regulations. A comparison of the annual volume of executive-made rules and regulations before 1900 with its counterpart today illustrates this point.[3] What modern legislator can or does take the trouble to read the enormous tome which comprises the budget?

In many fields of legislation the laws are intelligible only to the expert. Even a minister must look to consultative councils for expert advice. In France there are more than two hundred of these consultative councils attached to the various ministeries.[4]

Of all the advisory councils where the executive may obtain aid, the Conseil d'Etat is by far the most important. The Conseil has specialists in many fields and is well fitted for its consultative task. The scope of consultation varies from relatively minor administrative problems to government bills. Since 1945, all government bills have been submitted to the Conseil, which examines them for correct legal form.

The continuing rise of the state's role in economic and social life and the delegation by parliaments to the executive and to experts of many matters formerly covered by statute are general movements affecting most Western democracies. In France these long-range movements are reinforced by particular factors. One such factor, that of ministerial instability, has been particularly noticeable since the end of the First World War. The lack of a stable majority for carrying out a legislative policy led the French interwar parliament at times to "delegate" sweeping legislative powers to the executive, who issued "decree-laws" drafted by expert committees attached to ministerial departments or by the bureau of the president of the Council of Ministers.

Another factor is the position of the French civil service, which has long been large and powerful. During a cabinet crisis, the French will continually remind a foreign observer that the absence of a government is not very important because the administration carries on. Indeed, there is a French saying which contains much truth, "We are not governed, but administered." The administration is, within limits, ready to serve any government and, in fact, almost any form of government. The whole of the administration is run by several thousand career men, who form an elite. Though not identifiable with any political party, they have definite class interests. They are recruited, with rare exceptions, from the middle class, often from the sons of civil servants. They are further knit together by strong educational, economic, and social ties.[5]

At the peak of the bureaucracy are about four hundred and fifty members of the "three great corps": the Conseil d'Etat, the Inspection of Finance, and the Court of Accounts. Although these people are willing to serve almost anyone, a government would find it difficult, if not impossible, to carry out policies which ran counter to the wishes or the interests of the "three great corps." [6] Indeed, many governments are too unstable to risk alienating these people and many ministers would find it difficult to manage the affairs entrusted to them without the aid of experts in their departments.

Being somewhat of an intermediary between the Council of Ministers and the active administration, and largely independent of either, the Conseil d'Etat is in a position to exert its influence on both. The spirit of the Conseil permeates the whole of the administration, not only by means of the Conseil's role as technical counselor but also through its judicial role. Like the role of technical counselor, the judicial role has evolved not from any Cartesian principle but on the basis of empirical necessity.

The judicial function of the Conseil is the result of special circumstances operating at the time of the Revolution. Since 1790 the French courts have been barred from interfering in administration and have been forbidden to try government officials for any acts connected with their duties. This prohibition was derived from an interpretation of the doctrine of separation of powers, which originated with Montesquieu's alleged misinterpretation of the English constitution.[7] It was given more precise form by members of the National Assembly of 1789, who wanted to prevent the ordinary courts from meddling in administrative affairs, as had been the case with the sovereign courts during the *ancien régime*. As a consequence, the law August 16–24, 1790, prohibited the ordinary courts from trying cases in which the public administration or its agents were involved. This prohibition was repeated in various laws and constitutions between 1790 and 1799 and is found in Article 75 of the Constitution of the Consulate.

Because the courts were prohibited from interfering with the administration, the administration became judge of its own cause in the event of conflicts between citizens and the administration or its agents. Beginning in 1800 such conflicts came under the jurisdiction of the Conseil d'Etat, although the Conseil could grant permission, which it did only rarely, to the injured party to prosecute the agents of the administration before the ordinary courts. Article 75 remained on the statute books until 1870, providing the administration and its agents with special rights not possessed by ordinary citizens.

The recognition that the citizen injured by an illegal administrative act should have a remedy led to the development of the Conseil into a court having a definite jurisdiction. Suits of citizens against the administration came to be tried by the Conseil d'Etat or by inferior administrative courts, generally the Councils of Prefecture in the departments. All other types of litigation fell within the ordinary jurisdiction, which is comprised of a network of civil, criminal, and commercial courts with the Court of Cassation at its head.

The development of a separate administrative jurisdiction is without parallel in common law countries which possess a single jurisdiction for all types of cases. The recent growth of administrative agencies with quasi-judicial powers has, however, led some jurists in Great Britain and the United States to advocate the creation of central administrative courts more or less analogous to the Conseil d'Etat. That it is possible today for some to regard this French institution as a worthy model for imitation is owing to its development, particularly during the Third Republic, into a court which offers positive guarantees to the citizen against the arbitrary or unjust action of the administration and affords guarantees to the administration against undue interference by ordinary courts.

Still another point on which the critics of the British and American system have dwelt is that a common law judge usually possesses little or no experience with problems faced by administrators and in many cases has the average citizen's distrust of "bureaucrats" and "bureaucratic methods." In fact judges have often circumvented, altered, or delayed administrative policies. In Britain this has occasionally led to the insertion of a clause in legislative enactments precluding ordinary judicial review.[8] In France the existence of a separate jurisdiction has averted many of the inconveniences of the Anglo-American system. Members of the Conseil possess administrative experience; they are specialized in administrative law and are cognizant of the methods and problems of the administrator. If this specialized knowledge has prevented an excessive curbing of the administration, it has also avoided excessive leniency in judging the administration for its faults. The Conseil has succeeded in imbuing the administration with a respect for legality of action, though the Conseil as an administrative court has been aided in this task by its role of technical counselor of the government.

THE CONSEIL D'ETAT AS TECHNICAL COUNSELOR OF THE GOVERNMENT

The function of the Conseil d'Etat as technical counselor has varied since 1800 depending on the form of government in power. The extent of the powers of the Conseil as technical counselor has been dependent on the organization of the executive power and on the state of opinion of every new regime, a change in regime usually placing the institutions of the previous one in an aura of disrepute. In 1814 the Conseil was in disfavor because of the large role it had played under the Consulate and Empire. Therefore, from 1815 to 1830 the role of the Conseil as technical counselor was almost nonexistent. With the advent of the July Monarchy the fortunes of the Conseil began to rise, and this upward trend continued until 1869 under Louis Napoleon's "liberal Empire."

During the Second Republic the Conseil was endowed with some legislative power, drafting government bills, with the exception of finance bills and emergency legislation. It was originally conceived as an auxiliary of the executive, which had always been its traditional role, but the hostility between Louis Napoleon and the National Assembly caused the Assembly, which elected Councilors of State, to employ the Conseil as a check upon the presidency.[9] The election of the members of the Conseil by the Assembly marked a break in precedent; before 1848, the members of the Conseil had always been appointed by the executive. The 1848 precedent was to be adopted again in the early years of the Third Republic, because a majority of the Assembly was opposed to Thiers.[10]

After the *coup d'état* of 1851, when Louis Napoleon seized power, the appointment of members of the Conseil by the executive was resumed. Louis Napoleon restored to the Conseil a large degree of the importance it had had under his illustrious forebear. The Conseil drafted all legislative bills and all amendments suggested by the Legislative Assembly; no bill or amendment could be discussed by the Legislative Assembly without the prior approval of the Conseil d'Etat. But, with the advent of the "liberal Empire" in 1869, the Legislative Assembly was given the right to initiate and discuss bills without their prior examination by the Conseil d'Etat.

After the fall of the Empire in 1870, the Conseil was again in disrepute, as it had been in 1814, and the participation of the Conseil d'Etat in the legislative process during the Third Republic was accordingly small. That an institution such as the Conseil d'Etat, which is not directly responsible to the electorate, should have an essential part in the legislative process was thought to be incompatible with parliamentary democracy. Since 1870, the role of the Conseil in legislative matters has been advisory.

In addition to its legislative role, the Conseil d'Etat plays a part in the formulation of executive-made rules and regulations, known generally as delegated legislation in Britain and the United States.[11] These rules and regulations are inferior to a law (*loi*), which taken in its strict sense refers to an act of the French parliament. This has led to the establishment of the doctrine of the "hierarchy of laws and decrees." At the top of the hierarchy is constitutional law, followed by statutory enactments of parliament, though the superiority of the former over the latter is largely theoretical because there is no power in France to force the parliament to adhere to the letter or spirit of the Constitution. Next in the hierarchy come regulations of public administration (*règlements d'administration publique*), which are issued by the executive in execution of a law, on the "invitation" of parliament. The proviso contained in a law that the law will be executed by a regulation of public administration is considered by some French jurists to be an "invitation" to the executive and not a grant of power, because the executive in France possesses an autonomous rule-making power independent of any parliamentary permission. Thus, if a parliamentary "invitation" were lacking, this type of regulation could be issued in the form of an ordinary decree (*décret*).

Following the regulation of public administration in the hierarchy is a decree in the form of a regulation of public administration (*décret en forme d'un règlement d'administration publique*), a decree in the Conseil d'Etat (*décret en Conseil d'Etat*), and an ordinary decree (*décret*).[12] The principle of hierarchy requires that a lower form cannot be used where a higher form is required, nor can a provision of a lower form amend or violate the provision of a form above it. What form is required is largely dependent on the subject matter; for example, the establishment of the budget or new taxes require a law.[13] Which agency will collect the new taxes and by what means is an administrative matter and normally the subject of a regulation of public administration or an ordinary decree.

The Conseil enforces strict adherence to the principle of hierarchy, except in the case where a law violates a constitutional law.[14] However, the main brunt of enforcement of the principle of hierarchy falls on the judicial section of the Conseil rather than on the administrative sections; the latter can only warn against irregularities whereas the former can annul them. Of the above forms, the regulation of public administration, the decree in the form of a regulation of public administration, and a decree in the Conseil d'Etat are always submitted to the Conseil d'Etat for examination. If the executive fails to submit these types of regulations and decrees to the Conseil, in its capacity as technical counselor, they can be annulled by the judicial section of the Conseil for *ultra vires* on the ground of failure to observe procedures required by law.

The most important of the executive-made regulations and decrees is the regulation of public administration. The complexity of modern legislation has limited the area over which the details of execution can be covered by a law. Therefore the establishment of the details of execution has more and more been left to regulations of public administration. A law on the statute books is meaningless unless the execution is adequate and the agency of execution is sufficient to cope with the task. It has been charged that during the Third Republic, the drafting bureaus in the ministries and the Conseil d'Etat circumvented, by faulty execution, social legislation with which they were out of sympathy.[15] In the same manner the Conseil tried to moderate the application of the law on separation of church and state of 1905 by regulations of public administration.

Because the role of the Conseil in these matters is, in principle, secret, only a member of an administrative section of the Conseil could accurately say to what extent the Conseil can impose a policy contrary to that of the legislator. The literature on this aspect is practically nonexistent. I have been able to give only some examples of what is alleged to take place.

Every active member of the Conseil belongs to a section,

which is the basic internal unit of the body. There are now five sections in the Conseil, four devoted to the administrative work of the Conseil and one to the judicial. Today the judicial section is much larger than any of the administrative sections; about one half of the members of the Conseil are attached to the judicial section while the four administrative sections share the other half.

The administrative sections are always prepared, at the behest of a minister or some official delegated by a minister, to give advice concerning administrative problems, to interpret laws and regulations, or to determine what are the legal rules in force concerning a certain subject. Administrators are not required to solicit the advice of the Conseil on any of these matters, but do so for their own convenience. Members of the Conseil are often detached from their sections to serve as cabinet chiefs for a minister, as directors-general of ministerial departments, or in other high administrative posts. In this matter the Conseil operates as a reservoir of trained personnel that can be called upon to fill important posts in the administration. Without being detached from the Conseil, members are often invited to take part in the work of legislative drafting committees and other committees in the ministerial departments.

The membership of the Conseil is divided into three general ranks. They are, in order of importance, Councilors of State, Maîtres des Requêtes, and Auditors. As has been mentioned above, the first two ranks go back some six centuries. The rank of Auditor was a Bonapartist invention originating under the Consulate. At first the number of Auditors was small, but by 1814, at the end of the Empire, there were almost four hundred. The auditorship was then used as a school for administrators. Since 1814 the conception of the auditorship has been less grandiose; Auditors are today the main source of recruitment for Maîtres des Requêtes and eventually Councilors of State. During the Third Republic advancement on the basis of seniority became customary. Advancement by seniority, combined with *de facto* permanence of tenure, makes it difficult for the Conseil to be influenced by pressure from the outside. As will be seen, the Conseil in 1872 was not conceived as an independent body, but rather evolved into one. Without its independence from government pressure, the development of the judicial section of the Conseil into a respected court is difficult to conceive.

THE CONSEIL D'ETAT AS AN ADMINISTRATIVE COURT

French administrative law (*droit administratif*) can be defined simply as the rules which govern the organization and operation of the administration. The adjudication of conflicts arising from the organization and operation of the administration (*contentieux administratif*) is only a part of French administrative law, that part with which the Conseil d'Etat as the highest administrative court is concerned.

The view of the English-speaking world toward French administrative law has been long influenced by the famous constitutional writer Albert V. Dicey. In view of Dicey's great influence, it will be instructive to examine briefly his views, for they point up the great strides in the development of the Conseil as a court during the first part of the Third Republic. In his well-known *Introduction to the Study of the Law of the Constitution*, the first edition of which appeared in 1885, Dicey argued persuasively that French administrative law was incompatible with the English rule of law. Between 1885 and 1915 this book went through eight editions and Dicey's interpretation was generally accepted, even though before the turn of the century there was in English at least one account which differed from his [16] and after 1900 there were many who criticized his views. Although Dicey expanded his section on French administrative law, he maintained throughout all the editions his earlier view, in spite of familiarity with the writings of contemporary French administrative lawyers.[17] It is only now that the last vestiges of Dicey's influence are being eradicated.[18] Instead of following the customary path of pillorying Dicey for being wrong, it is more instructive to determine why and to what extent he was mistaken.

There are several reasons which help to explain Dicey's attitude. First, he considered administrative law as a continental system and denied, until he recanted in 1915, that Britain had any similar body of law. Second, Dicey denied, rightly, that the Conseil d'Etat was a court in the English sense, but he was led to conclude, wrongly, that the Conseil could not provide proper judicial safeguards. Third, his knowledge of the historical origin and early character of the Conseil greatly conditioned his view of the Conseil of the Third Republic and led him to depreciate the great transformation which took place then.[19] In the later editions of the *Law of the Constitution,* Dicey admitted that the Conseil was developing into a court in the accepted sense. Several writers have questioned whether Dicey's views concerning French administrative adjudication were valid as early as 1872, the date when the decisions of the Conseil ceased to require executive approval.

In 1885, when the first edition appeared, the transformation of French administrative adjudication was still largely in the future. It was possible for Dicey to ask whether or not the Conseil had the independence requisite for a judicial body because, only six years before, ten Councilors of State had been dismissed for not being in sympathy with the government. Legally, members of the Conseil held office at the pleasure of the government.[20] At that time it was difficult to foresee that by the end of the century the independence of the members of the Conseil would be tacitly recognized. Dicey also had to rely on books of administrative law such as those of Théophile Ducrocq, Léon Aucoc, and Anselme Batbie, all originally published during the Second Empire; such sources might easily have led him to regard the judicial activities of the Conseil as merely a continuation of the administrative power.

It was only in 1887 that the first volume of Edouard Laferrière's monumental *Traité de la juridiction administrative* appeared. The treatise of Laferrière, Vice-President of the Conseil d'Etat, was not only an orderly and reasoned description of the body of administrative adjudication as it existed in 1887, which he was the first to supply, but it was also a foundation on which to build. Before 1889 the ministerial departments still performed functions considered as judicial. Anyone injured by an administrative act had first to seek redress from the ministerial departments or from the Councils of Prefecture. The latter satisfied more nearly the criteria for a court, but the ministerial departments were judging cases to which they were a party. Appeal was always possible to the Conseil d'Etat, which before the celebrated *Cadot* decision of 1889 [21] considered the ministerial decisions as regular judicial decisions. Laferrière, in his treatise two years before, had called for the abandonment of this jurisprudence.

Thus, even though the Conseil d'Etat was given the final power of decision by the law of 1872, until 1889 the active administration still had a part in the judicial process. Such a feature could only confirm Dicey's suspicions. Another feature that repelled Dicey was the special position of civil servants in France. The ordinary courts could not try a civil servant for service-connected faults. Such cases had to be brought before the Conseil d'Etat, and since at this time the state was not pecuniarily responsible, with certain exceptions, the most important of which was damages caused by public works, no redress was possible for any damage suffered by the plaintiff. In Britain and the United States, the civil servant could be held pecuniarily responsible for any illegal act, even if committed on the orders of a superior. Therefore Dicey concluded that the citizen was better protected from illegal administrative action in common law countries than in France.

In my opinion, Dicey's views in 1885 on French administrative adjudication, though perhaps too heavily weighted in favor of its less attractive aspects, are not far from the truth. Unfortunately

Dicey never altered in the later editions the basic assumptions of the 1885 edition, even though he admitted somewhat cautiously that progress had been made.

During the Third Republic, the jurisprudence of the Conseil became increasingly liberal on both the grounds for receiving and judging the pleas of *ultra vires*. At the turn of the century the Conseil recognized the general pecuniary responsibility of the state for damages caused by the administration. In the twentieth century the Conseil applied certain principles of equity to contracts between the administration and the citizen. In short, the Conseil gave better protection to the citizen than the civil courts could have done, because the Conseil was free to develop administrative law in accordance with modern needs. French administrative jurisprudence has followed a development familiar to common law lawyers; it is case law and uncodified, unlike French civil and criminal law.

It was because of the development of the Conseil's jurisprudence that the segment of opinion opposing the existence of two orders of courts finally disappeared at the end of the nineteenth century. There had been since the fall of the First Empire a movement for the abolition of the administrative jurisdiction. This movement was at its peak between 1818 and 1830; its arguments against the administrative jurisdiction were presented most effectively by the Duc de Broglie in an article in the *Revue française* of 1828. During the July Monarchy several bills were introduced to curtail or to suppress entirely the jurisdiction of the Conseil, but none of them found favor with the majority of the Assembly. Even de Tocqueville, as a member of a committee to study the reform of the Conseil d'Etat during the July Monarchy, voted against the suppression of the administrative jurisdiction.[22] Later, during the debate on the reorganization of the Conseil d'Etat in 1872, which will be treated in the next chapter, there was an attempt to abolish the administrative jurisdiction. It is to this reorganization that we now turn.

2

THE STRUCTURE OF THE CONSEIL D'ETAT, 1872-1940

ON September 4, 1870, two days after the surrender of the encircled French army and the Emperor at Sedan, the Government of National Defense came into existence at the Palais Bourbon, with the support of the mob. The Bonapartes were dethroned and the Government of National Defense, composed mainly of deputies from Paris, became the master of war-torn France. In the days that followed, the Legislative Assembly and the Senate were dissolved. In the general disbanding of the institutions of the Second Empire, the Conseil d'Etat followed shortly.

On September 15, a decree suspended from their functions all members of the Conseil d'Etat of the Second Empire (Article 1). The same decree (Article 2) set up a provisional commission to replace the Conseil d'Etat until a new Conseil could be reorganized by a future Constituent Assembly. The newly and temporarily established provisional commission was to expedite all urgent administrative and judicial matters that were normally handled by the Conseil d'Etat. The provisional nature of the commission was emphasized by its smallness; it was composed of eight Councilors of State, ten Maîtres des Requêtes, and twelve Auditors. The Conseil d'Etat of the Second Empire had contained 170 regular members compared with the thirty of the provisional commission.

The provisional commission was divided into three sections,[1] two to handle the administrative work and one to perform the judicial function. The members of the judicial section were also members of one of the administrative sections. Since the administrative work was given precedence over the judicial work, the judicial section, from its organization until the end of 1871, was able to judge only 459 cases, or about a quarter of those registered. Thus, a considerable backlog of unjudged cases accumulated.

The administrative work, which was more pressing than the judicial work owing to the problems created by the war and its aftermath, was kept up to date thanks to a considerable effort on the part of the commission. During the period September 19, 1870, to December 31, 1871, the two administrative sections examined 19,636 matters, but slightly over 16,000 of these were concerned with civil and military pensions, which were relatively unimportant. Of the approximately 3,500 other matters the most important were eight regulations of public administration drafted by the Conseil creating new taxes.[2]

PARLIAMENTARY HISTORY OF THE LAW REORGANIZING
THE CONSEIL D'ETAT

The end of the war with Germany enabled the National Assembly, elected on February 8, 1871, to turn to the organization of the new regime. Jean Dufaure, the minister of justice in the provisional government of Adolphe Thiers, presented a government bill on June 1, 1871, for the reorganization of the Conseil d'Etat. The report preceding the bill (*exposé des motifs*) called for the organization of a *provisional* Conseil d'Etat;[3] the Conseil was to be reorganized when the new constitution was drafted and the future organization of the judiciary was decided upon. But the provisional organization of the Conseil at this time was necessary, the report declared, owing to the inadequacy of the provisional commission.[4] When the constitution would be drafted and the nature of the regime decided could not be foreseen. The government, by proposing a provisional reorganization, recognized the interrelation between the structure of the Conseil d'Etat and the form of government, and the necessity of harmonizing the Conseil with the judicial and administrative organization of the country.

The government bill was composed almost entirely of articles taken from the laws of 1845 and 1849 on the Conseil d'Etat. The utilization of these two laws was also calculated to appease the two main factions of the Assembly, the monarchists and the republicans. Features of these two laws formed the main lines of the government bill and were to constitute the salient parts of the law of May 24, 1872, on the Conseil, though not in the manner conceived by the government. Before turning to the government bill, the main features of both the July Monarchy and Second Republic laws on the Conseil should be understood.

The law of July 19, 1845, which was almost fifteen years in its formulation, was the definitive law on the Conseil of the July Monarchy, although by the time it was passed the monarchy was in the last three years of its life. Under this law the king appointed the members of the Conseil d'Etat; they could be removed by a decree of the council of ministers. The Conseil d'Etat took part in the legislative and rule-making process only on the invitation of the legislative and executive powers, with the exception that the law required that all regulations of public administration be submitted to the Conseil for examination. In judicial matters all decisions needed the signature of the king and the minister of justice to become effective (*justice retenue*). This, of course, could be and was a source of abuse. It gave the king an effective veto over all decisions that tended to embarrass the government. In addition, under the famous Article 75,[5] an ordinary court could not summon an agent of the administration for an act relating to his function without the permission of the Conseil d'Etat. Even assuming that the Conseil was willing to grant permission, its will was without effect unless the decision was signed by the king and the minister of justice.

With the Second Republic, the Conseil d'Etat ceased to be

the classic auxiliary of the executive power and became instead a sort of right hand of the legislature. The members of the Conseil were elected by the National Assembly for six-year terms, instead of being appointed by the executive.[6] The Conseil also had a legislative function defined by the Constitution of the Second Republic: "The Conseil d'Etat is consulted on government bills, which according to law must be submitted for preliminary examination, and on bills of parliamentary initiative that the assembly sends to it."[7] For legislative matters the Conseil served as a drafting bureau. In judicial matters the Conseil was given definitive power of judgment (*justice déléguée*), that is, its decisions were to be final and effective without the signature of the chief executive or a minister. The law of March 8, 1849 provided for the establishment of a Tribunal of Conflicts, composed of members in equal number from the Conseil d'Etat and the Court of Cassation, the highest civil court. The Tribunal of Conflicts decided which jurisdiction was competent in the event of a conflict of jurisdiction. A conflict of jurisdiction arose when a prefect contested the right of a court of the ordinary jurisdiction to try a case on the ground that the administrative jurisdiction was competent. Such conflicts, before 1849, were removed to the Conseil d'Etat for judgment. This type of procedure gave the Conseil an opportunity to encroach upon the ordinary jurisdiction, and in order to prevent such encroachment the Tribunal of Conflicts, composed of members from both orders of courts, was created. In case of a tie in the vote of the Tribunal, the deciding vote was to be cast by the minister of justice.

The government bill, which Dufaure presented in 1871, was a combination of certain features from each of the two laws discussed above. It provided for the creation of a Tribunal of Conflicts composed of four members from each the Conseil d'Etat and the Court of Cassation. As under the Second Republic, the minister of justice was to cast the deciding vote in case of a tie.

STRUCTURE OF THE CONSEIL, 1872-1940   19

In judicial matters the Conseil was to be given the final power of decision (*justice déléguée*), as provided for by the law of 1849.

The members of the Conseil were to be named by the chief of the executive power, then Thiers, and dismissed by a decree of the council of ministers, imitating the law of 1845 of the July Monarchy. The government and legislature could, if they chose, submit bills to the scrutiny of the Conseil, but this was entirely optional. The bill further provided that the Conseil must be consulted on all regulations of public administration, a feature common to both the July Monarchy and the Second Republic.

In the National Assembly, a special committee of fifteen, under the presidency of Saint-Marc-Girardin, was chosen to examine the bill. Of the fifteen, eleven were affiliated with parties on the right and four with parties on the left.[8] The secretary of the committee was Paul de Rémusat and the reporter[9] (*rapporteur*) was Anselme Batbie. The Duc Albert de Broglie, then ambassador to London and shortly to become the recognized leader of the Orleanist group, and the Marquis de Chasseloup-Laubat, who had been the reporter for the law of 1845, were also members of the committee. However the most influential member was its reporter, Batbie, who had been for many years a professor at the Faculty of Law of the University of Paris and whose book on administrative law[10] was considered at that time as a definitive treatment of the subject.

Batbie presented his first report, which embodied the decisions of the committee, to the Assembly on January 29, 1872. The committee had decided not to adopt the qualification "provisional" proposed by the government bill but took the position that a law is a law and, whether provisional or definitive, another law is necessary to change it. In the words of Batbie's report: "Our work, in effect, will be definitive or provisional depending on whether it is maintained or changed. This depends on circumstances of which we are not the masters."[11]

The report defended the separation of jurisdictions: first, because the judgment of cases involving the administration requires a specialized knowledge which ordinary judges seldom possess, and second, because the ordinary judges, who were irremovable, would interfere with the administrative process. The latter objection, which went back to the Constituent Assembly of 1789, was the original reason for the separation of the administrative and judicial powers. A strong minority of the committee, led by the Duc de Broglie, had opposed the establishment of separate jurisdictions. The Duc de Broglie proposed, as had his father in an article in the *Revue française* in 1828,[12] to abolish the administrative jurisdiction and let the ordinary courts decide cases where there was a conflict between an individual and the administration. The liberal position of this Orleanist family was reinforced by their memory of a decision of the Conseil d'Etat regarding the confiscation of their property during the Second Empire.[13]

The committee, conforming to the government bill, proposed to give the Conseil d'Etat the power of final decision and also to establish a Tribunal of Conflicts to decide conflicts of jurisdiction between the two orders of courts. Contrary to the government bill, the committee opposed letting the minister of justice cast the deciding vote in case of a tie. The committee foresaw—erroneously, as later events showed—that ties would be frequent because the Councilors of State would vote for their jurisdiction while the members from the Court of Cassation would do likewise. The minister of justice, the committee feared, would vote according to the political aspects of the case. Besides, rarely has the minister of justice a knowledge of jurisprudence and his other duties would prevent him from devoting much time to the Tribunal. Also, the report continued, ministers of justice are subject to frequent change and this might cause abrupt changes in jurisprudence. The committee proposed to solve the difficulty by forming the Tribunal with three members from the Conseil d'Etat, three from the Court of Cassation, and three elected by the National Assembly.

The most important change made by the committee in the government bill, and the one which led to the most controversy, affected the method of choosing Councilors of State. The government bill had proposed that they be named by the chief of the executive power, as under the July Monarchy, while the committee proposed that they be elected by the National Assembly, as under the Second Republic. The majority of the committee, Orleanist in sympathy, did not want to see the appointive power fall into the hands of Thiers.

The committee bill provided for a President of the Conseil d'Etat, chosen from among the Councilors of State. The government bill had proposed a Vice-President chosen by the chief of the executive power also from among the Councilors of State; the presidency was to fall to the minister of justice. This was another feature of the bill, as amended by the committee, designed to limit the power of the executive over the Conseil.

The legislative function of the Conseil was to be strictly limited; on this point, both the government and the committee were in agreement. The Conseil could be asked to draft or give advice on bills, but only on the invitation of parliament or the executive. The report stated that the functions of the Conseil were to be "principally administrative and, only by exception, legislative." [14] A member of the committee, the Marquis de Chasseloup-Laubat had proposed a bill, which would have given the Conseil a considerable consultative power over legislation,[15] but his proposal had been rejected by the other members of the committee.

The first debate on the bill took place in the National Assembly on February 19, 1872, at Versailles.[16] In speeches before the National Assembly Antonin Lefèvre-Pontalis and Claude-Marie Raudot, a partisan of decentralization, wanted to do away with the Conseil d'Etat entirely. "England," Raudot told the Assembly, "has no Conseil d'Etat." [17] He held the Conseil responsible for all kinds of regulations and restrictions on individual liberty, and particularly on economic liberty:

The Conseil d'Etat is the fortress of centralization. . . . The destruction of this fortress would be worth hundreds of millions yearly, which individuals would create in new wealth because they would have complete liberty of action, while with your present system of regulation, one is tied hand and foot at every turn.[18]

Gambetta, speaking for the radical republicans, took issue sharply with Raudot. For a country organized like France, Gambetta thought the Conseil d'Etat a necessity; it was a uniquely French institution, one of the best inherited from the French monarchy. But he considered its organization at this time to be premature because the Conseil d'Etat was an auxiliary of the executive power, and the organization of that power was as yet provisional:

It is necessary that this Conseil d'Etat have an organization perfectly harmonious with the central power, and with the form of this power. . . . That which would be logical, would be to start by organizing this power, and to create afterwards the institutions which are just and adequate to it.[19]

Gambetta urged the Assembly to reject the bill and avoid passing to a second reading.

Batbie, the reporter, asked the Assembly to pass to the second reading in a speech in which he characterized the Conseil as being an essentially administrative body. However, Batbie also recognized the necessity of having an institution to aid the Assembly in its legislative task. "The Conseil d'Etat," Batbie declared, "such as we propose to organize it . . . is not, properly speaking, a political body; it is an auxiliary for the preparation of laws, to which one can optionally send for examination bills emanating from governmental initiative or from parliamentary initiative."[20] Dufaure, the minister of justice, speaking for the government, likewise urged the Assembly to pass to a second reading. He stressed the fact that the government and the committee were in accord on all the main issues, except the mode of naming Councilors of State. Then the Assembly, by a voice vote, decided to pass to the second reading. Thus this ancient monarchical institution, which had been remodeled by Napoleon, was accepted by the National Assembly as one of the institutions of the Third Republic.

The second reading started on April 23 and was continued on the 29th and 30th, and on the 1st, 2d, and 3d of May. The importance attributed to this bill was emphasized by the fact that, on the parliamentary calendar, it was given priority over an important bill reorganizing the army. At the opening of the session on the 23d, Paul-Louis Target and seven other members of the Assembly sponsored a substitute bill, which proposed:

Until the Assembly has decided on the political constitution of the country, the decree of September 15, 1870, will continue in effect.

The government is authorized to raise, according to the needs of the service, the number of Councilors of State to sixteen, that of Maîtres des Requêtes to twenty, that of Auditors to twenty-four.[21]

This bill would have merely doubled the membership of the provisional commission. Target, defending his bill, reminded the Assembly that a majority of the committee on decentralization was in favor of abolishing the Councils of Prefecture which were, among other things, administrative courts subordinate to the Conseil d'Etat. If the Councils of Prefecture were going to be suppressed then it was needless to organize definitively the Conseil d'Etat, argued Target. On the request of Batbie, the substitute bill was referred to the committee for further examination.

On the 29th, Batbie, on behalf of the committee, asked the Assembly to reject the substitute bill. Then Batbie touched off an uproar in the Assembly by accusing the legitimists of the extreme right and the republicans of forming a parliamentary coalition to pass the Target measure and thereby kill the committee bill. This, in effect, was what had happened. The center was astonished to see such bitter political opponents as Jacques Rivet, a republican, and Amédée Lefèvre-Pontalis, a legitimist and one of the sponsors of the substitute bill, defend the measure. The latter responded to Batbie's accusations: "If he finds united on the amendment under discussion the names which I regret are not always together, it is proof that the same light can radiate at the same time on different sides of the Assembly." [22] Was this coalition of dissidents, motivated by the "same light," to prove strong enough to carry the substitute bill?

The coalition was weakened by the fact that many of the republicans preferred to follow Dufaure, the republican minister of justice, than to vote with their bitter enemies. The substitute bill was defeated by 364 to 239. Gambetta abstained, which might appear surprising in view of the fact that at the first reading he had shown himself favorable to a solution such as the substitute bill proposed. But the responsible leaders of the left did not desire to embarrass the Thiers's government in company with the legitimists.[23]

The Assembly then proceeded to discuss the bill article by article. The debate on Article 3, concerning the nomination of Councilors of State, was the bitterest, for it was the main point of difference between the government bill and that of the committee. On the 30th, Benjamin Bardoux and Charles Bertauld introduced an amendment to give the chief of the executive power the right to appoint Councilors of State. Bardoux, in a didactic speech, defended the amendment. Election of Councilors by the Assembly, he claimed, would make the Conseil d'Etat a political body and would also violate the principle of separation of powers laid down by Montesquieu.

Appeals to logic, to the doctrine of separation of powers, and to tradition were of no avail. The center did not wish to see the power of appointment fall into the hands of Thiers. Hostility between Thiers and the royalists had deepened since the beginning of 1872. The most important positions in the cabinet were held by republicans, a situation irritating to the royalists. Here was a chance to strike back at Thiers; the royalists would deprive him of the right to appoint Councilors of State.

During the debates it was not long before the fictitious issues of separation of powers and of whether or not the Conseil was to become a political body were dropped. Audren de Kerdrel, one of the leaders of the legitimists, expressed the thoughts of many of the royalists when, opposing the amendment, he said:

The executive power listens above all to the men who live in Paris. Moreover, let me say that among these men of the government there are those who have served too many regimes (lively applause on the right and right center) and whose devotion to themselves is not for me a sufficient guarantee of their devotion to the country (renewed applause).[24]

These remarks were obviously meant to include Thiers.

The government offensive in support of the amendment was led by the minister of justice, Dufaure. With the exception of 1848, the executive had always appointed the members of the Conseil, affirmed the minister of justice. Appointment by the executive would also insure the removability of Councilors of State; but, Dufaure further asserted, Councilors would tend to become irremovable if elected by the National Assembly. If the Assembly insisted on naming the Councilors, Dufaure painted a dark picture of what would happen:

The Conseil d'Etat becomes derelict in its duty; it becomes unfaithful to the Assembly which named it; it wounds the Assembly by its inconsiderateness; it refuses to execute the laws of the Assembly; who will be responsible! [?] (Exclamations on the right.) [25]

However, Dufaure reasoned, if the executive appoints the Councilors, they will be responsible to the executive, and the executive is responsible to the Assembly. Another reason why the executive should be allowed to appoint Councilors is that the consultative function of the Conseil makes it the natural auxiliary of the executive and therefore Councilors should be responsible to the executive.

These arguments were attacked by the reporter, Batbie. He ridiculed the idea of the Conseil opposing the Assembly which had named it. Agreeing with Dufaure that the Conseil advises the executive, he pointed out that the executive is not obligated to take the advice of the Conseil.

When the vote was taken, the amendment was defeated 338 to 316. Voting for the amendment were all the republicans, the left center, and all the ministers except one (de Larcy, who abstained). The right center and the legitimists had carried the day. The vote was interpreted as a rebuke to the government. The newspaper *Le Figaro*, of the extreme right, gleefully called it a serious check to that "consummate logician" Dufaure, the government, and the left.[26] The *Journal des Débats* and *Le Temps*, both conservative, considered the vote "regrettable." [27] *Le Temps* commented that happily there was a possibility that the power would be restored during the third reading. On May 5 the *Débats* reported "from worthy sources" that Thiers was not pleased with the vote, in fact so displeased that he would resign unless the right of appointment were restored.[28] The *République française*, Gambettist, predicted that the right would be restored during the third reading.[29]

On May 23, at the beginning of the third reading, Batbie, on behalf of the committee, read an additional report to the Assembly. In Batbie's words:

Your committee, however, after having submitted the bill to a new examination, has decided that the role of the executive could be extended, and it [the committee] has charged me to propose to you modifications *which are inspired by a spirit of conciliation*.[30]

What were the reasons for this "spirit of conciliation?" The committee had taken seriously Thiers's threatened resignation. Perhaps the committee thought that since the vote of May 3 on Article 3 had been so close, it would be unwise to force another test of strength, especially since the displeasure of Thiers was common currency. Actually, a compromise had taken place and Broglie, by his own admission, had acted as conciliator.[31] Thiers was still too valuable for the center and right to risk a conflict *à outrance*.

Batbie's report proposed to give the presidency of the Conseil to the minister of justice; the original bill of the committee had proposed that the president be elected by the Councilors of

State. The minister of justice was also to be given the presidency of the Tribunal of Conflicts with the right to cast the deciding vote in case of a tie. The Tribunal of Conflicts, according to the new proposal, was to be composed of nine members, three each from the Conseil d'Etat and the Court of Cassation, two elected by the original six, and the minister of justice. In the original committee bill there were to be three each from the Conseil d'Etat and the Court of Cassation, plus three elected by the National Assembly. These conciliatory proposals increased the influence of the executive over the Conseil through the agency of the minister of justice.

Evidently the compromise was satisfactory to Thiers because the government made no effort to oppose Article 3 during the vote, which took place the following day. Only the left remained dissatisfied over Article 3. The rest of the Assembly accepted the compromise proposals but "without enthusiasm." [32] With one important exception, and that concerning Article 3, the main features of the law of May 24, 1872, were to endure as the basic statute on the Conseil d'Etat throughout the Third Republic.

THE LAW OF MAY 24, 1872 [33]

The law provided for twenty-two Councilors of State, elected by the National Assembly for a term of nine years and renewed by thirds every three years. No one could be a Councilor of State unless he was at least thirty years of age. The law provided that membership in the Conseil d'Etat was incompatible with membership in the National Assembly or the management of a company subsidized by the State. The President of the Council of Ministers could, by a decree of the Council of Ministers, suspend a Councilor of State for two months. If, during this time, he was not dismissed by the National Assembly, he could return to his functions. Councilors of State were to have a vote in all the different branches of the Conseil to which they belonged. The Vice-President of the Conseil d'Etat, the minister of justice being President, was to be appointed by the President of the Republic from among the Councilors of State.

Next in rank after Councilors of State come the Maîtres des Requêtes. There were to be twenty-four Maîtres des Requêtes appointed by the President of the Republic by decree in the Council of Ministers and revocable in the same manner. One-third of the Maîtres des Requêtes had to be appointed from First Class Auditors. To be eligible, they must have attained the age of twenty-seven. They had a vote on all matters for which they were the reporters [34] and the right of discussion in all other matters. One of the Maîtres des Requêtes performed the function of Secretary-General of the bureau of the Conseil d'Etat.

The law provided for thirty Auditors divided into two classes, ten First Class Auditors and twenty Second Class Auditors. First Class Auditors were to be chosen exclusively by competitive examination from Second Class Auditors. In 1879, the competitive examination for First Class Auditors was dispensed with and they were appointed by the President of the Republic on the recommendation of the Vice-President and the Section Presidents of the Conseil from among Second Class Auditors. At the time of his appointment, a First Class Auditor had to be at least twenty-five years of age and not more than thirty.

Second Class Auditors were chosen by competitive examination. They had to be at least twenty-one years of age and not more than twenty-five. A Second Class Auditor could remain in his function for four years, at the end of which, if he had not received appointment as a First Class Auditor, he was transferred to a post in the civil service. Thus, the auditorship was supposed to serve two functions: it was a training school for administrators and a reservoir for furnishing personnel for the Conseil d'Etat. In the Conseil, Auditors were employed exclusively as reporters. They had a vote in the sections and the right of discussion in the Conseil's General Assembly on matters on which they were the reporters.

Second Class Auditors were unpaid. During the debates on the law in the National Assembly, François Limpérani, a member of the republican group, proposed that they be paid, but Batbie, on behalf of the committee, rejected the idea. The auditorship was considered as a training school for civil servants, and Batbie pointed out that the government did not pay the students at the universities. This restricted the candidates to those who could afford to spend four years without pay. However, any candidate who could pass the competitive examination was already the recipient of an education, usually in a Faculty of Law. Thus the lack of pay discriminated against candidates from lower middle-class families and worked in favor of candidates from the upper middle class and the nobility. At that time, few youths with working-class backgrounds received a *lycée* education, let alone education on a university level.

The competitive examination for appointment to Second Class Auditor was very difficult, especially after 1880 when the requirements were strictly applied. Examinations were to be conducted every year for the number of vacancies which existed. In the early years of the operation of the law, there were no examinations in some years because no vacancies existed. However, in practice, especially after subsequent legislation increased the number of Auditors, examinations were held annually, except during wartime. The law of 1872 made a special provision for Auditors of the Conseil d'Etat of the Second Empire and the provisional commission, which performed the duties of the Conseil d'Etat from September, 1870, until the law of 1872 went into effect, by relaxing the requirements of age for them. Also as a concession to these former Auditors, the law provided that for the first time, First Class Auditors would be chosen from among them. At the first examination, thirty-five Auditors competed for the ten places.[35]

The examination for Second Class Auditor, and, until 1879, for First Class Auditor, covered the following subjects: (1) French public and constitutional law, (2) administrative and judicial organization in France, and the history of administrative institutions since 1789, (3) administrative law, and (4) elements of political economy. Early in the twentieth century the candidate was also expected to have a knowledge of French civil law and public international law.[36] Candidates were required to have a degree in law or its equivalent. The competition included both oral and written examinations, and, under the system of scoring for the oral examination, the jury could take into account the appearance and character of the candidate. In the first examination, held in 1872, sixty-eight candidates competed for twenty places. In subsequent examinations there were usually five or six candidates competing for each vacancy, a proportion which remained about the same throughout the Third Republic.

In addition to the regular personnel, the law provided for fifteen Councilors of State in special service (*Conseillers d'Etat en service extraordinaire*), one from every ministerial department. These persons were included in the membership of the Conseil to air the opinion of the active administration and to provide first-hand knowledge of administrative problems. They were assigned to one of the administrative sections and had a vote on all matters pertaining to their department. They could not belong to the Judicial Section or take part in the judicial business of the Conseil. Councilors of State in special service held administrative posts; usually they were directors-general in one of the ministerial departments, and because of their regular duties, they seldom took part in the work of the Conseil, unless the matter under consideration was very important. Also, all cabinet ministers could take part in the nonjudicial work of the Conseil and they had a vote on all affairs concerning their ministries. In practice none ever exercised this right during the Third Republic. The minister of justice, as President of the Conseil d'Etat, could vote on any of the nonjudicial matters taken up by the Conseil; however, the minister of justice rarely took part in the work of the Conseil. On any given matter, the number of the nonregular members of the Conseil possessing the right to vote, such as Councilors of State in special service, ministers, and the minister of justice, was always inferior to the number of regular members. Thus, the Councilors of State in special service and the ministers could not secure favorable decisions from the Conseil unless several of the regular members were in agreement with them. This was, however, never an important factor because the Councilors in special service or the ministers rarely attended.

The work of the Conseil was carried out in its various internal branches—the sections, the Public Assembly, and the General Assembly. The law of 1872 provided for four sections, three administrative sections and a Judicial Section (*section du contentieux*). All matters which came to the Conseil were first submitted to a section for examination. Many important matters were carried from the section to the Public Assembly, for judicial matters, or the General Assembly, for administrative or legislative matters. The three administrative sections comprised the Sections of Interior, Finance, and Public Works. Matters concerning the various ministerial departments were divided among these three sections. For example, the Section of Finance handled all the matters coming from the Ministries of War, Navy, Finance, Merchant Marine, and Colonies.

In the General Assembly, which was concerned with important administrative and legislative matters, all Councilors of State were voting members. In this Assembly, the ministers and Councilors of State in special service had the right to vote on any matter pertaining to their department and could express their opinion on all others; the minister of justice, being ex officio President of the Conseil, could vote on all matters. Maîtres des Requêtes could vote on all matters of which they were the reporters and could express their opinion on all others.

The 1872 law required that all bills and regulations of public administration be submitted to the General Assembly. In addition, the administrative sections could submit to the General Assembly any matter they deemed of sufficient importance to merit examination by this body. The minister of justice (President) or the Vice-President also could order any matter to be taken to the General Assembly that they thought should be examined by that body.

The Judicial Section was composed of six Councilors of State plus the Vice-President, who served as that section's president. The assignment of Maîtres des Requêtes and Auditors among the sections was made by order of the minister of justice on the advice of the Vice-President; the number assigned to each section varied according to the needs of the service. In 1872 the Judicial Section employed approximately two fifths of the Maîtres des Requêtes and Auditors, this proportion increasing to about three fifths in 1939. The Public Assembly, which examined important judicial matters sent to it by the Judicial Section, was composed of all the Councilors of State of the Judicial Section, the Vice-President, and six other Councilors of State, two from each of the administrative sections, making a total of thirteen. It could not deliberate unless nine members were present. The accompanying diagram shows how the Conseil was organized by the law of 1872.

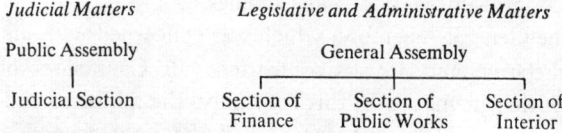

ORGANIZATION OF THE CONSEIL D'ETAT (LAW OF MAY 24, 1872)

On the legislative and administrative functions of the Conseil, Article 8 stated:

The Conseil d'Etat gives advice (1) on bills of parliamentary initiative that the National Assembly judges fit to send to it, (2) on bills of governmental initiative that a special decree orders submitted to it, (3) on drafts of decrees and, in general, on all the questions that are submitted to it by the President of the Republic or by the ministers. It is required to give its advice on all regulations of public administration and on all decrees in the form of a regulation of public administration. It exercises besides, until it be otherwise ordained, all functions that were conferred on the old Conseil d'Etat by laws or regulations which have not been abrogated.[37]

The importance and extent of these legislative and administrative functions will be taken up in later chapters.

Certain features of the law were never operative, such as the provision that Councilors of State could be charged by the government to defend bills, which the Conseil had examined, before the National Assembly. This provision envisioned Councilors of State defending any modifications made in bills by the Conseil and explaining to the Assembly the reason for such changes. A provision such as this, if operative, would have provided technical assistance to an Assembly whose knowledge of legal and technical intricacies was generally meager. The legislative assemblies, however, never shared with the authors of the act the thought that such a procedure was necessary, or even desirable.

On the judicial function, Article 9 of the law of 1872 provided:

The Conseil d'Etat sits definitively on all cases in matters of administrative adjudication, and on all requests of annulment for *ultra vires* directed against the acts of the diverse administrative authorities.[38]

The provision that the Conseil d'Etat "sits definitively" gave the Conseil the final power of decision over the cases of its resort. Prior to the enactment of Article 9, the signature of the executive on all decisions of the Conseil had been required before they had the force of law, except during the short-lived Conseil of the Second Republic. Heretofore, because the executive could refuse to sign the decision of the Conseil, there existed the possibility of abuse. Giving the Conseil d'Etat the power of independent judgment satisfied many of the liberal critics, like Gambetta, but as has been noted, there were those, like Raudot, who notwithstanding this provision wanted to suppress the administrative jurisdiction.

Carrying out the provisions of the law, the National Assembly on July 22, 24, 25, and 26, 1872, elected the Councilors of State. The majority of them were men with legal experience and many of them had been members of the Conseil d'Etat during the Second Empire. Twelve of those elected were on both the lists of the right and left.[39] Thiers picked from among those elected an advocate, Odilon Barrot, an old republican and one of the promoters of the political banquets of 1847, to be the first Vice-President of the Conseil d'Etat of the Third Republic. A third of the Councilors of State were to be elected every three years, so the men elected in the first election were chosen for terms of three, six, and nine years. The first election by the National Assembly, however, also proved to be the last.

SUBSEQUENT MODIFICATIONS DURING THE THIRD REPUBLIC

Before the term of the third of the Councilors of State elected for three years had expired, the system of election of Councilors by the Assembly was abandoned. In 1875, on the evening of February 24th, during the final stages of the debate on the constitutional bill relative to the organization of the public powers, Henri Wallon, Charles Gaslonde, and seven others proposed an amendment giving the President of the Republic the power to appoint Councilors of State. Of the nine sponsors of this amendment, five had voted against a similar provision in the law of 1872. On the following day, the 25th, the reporter announced that the committee had accepted the amendment and incorporated it into Article 4 of the constitutional bill. The acceptance of the amendment by the committee on the very day of the final vote, which was an unusual procedure, provoked sharp criticism from Raoul Duval and Claude-Marie Raudot on the grounds that the amendment was being rushed through without due consideration. But the opposition to the amendment came solely from the extreme right and the amendment passed by a vote of 467 to 46.[40] The text provided:

As vacancies occur after the promulgation of the present law, the President of the Republic appoints, in the Council of Ministers, the Councilors of State in ordinary service.

The Councilors of State thus chosen can be dismissed only by a decree approved by the Council of Ministers.[41]

The acceptance of the amendment by the center majority constituted a reversal of the position its members had held during the debates on the law of 1872. In 1872, the majority did not wish to see the appointive power fall into the hands of Thiers. Their hostility toward Thiers caused them to retain the power of appointment for themselves, although traditionally and logically it belonged to the executive. After the resignation of Thiers in 1873 and the elevation of Marshal MacMahon to the presidency, there was no reason for the right to maintain its former position.[42] Also, having lost control of the Assembly, the royalists could no longer hope to elect their own men to the Conseil and MacMahon could be relied upon to appoint men favorable to them. The amendment was also of a nature to satisfy MacMahon, who had been refused the right to appoint the life senators.[43] These were the deciding factors in the vote of the royalists. As for the left, it consistently maintained its position of 1872. Thiers himself voted for the bill along with Batbie and Audren de Kerdrel, two members who had led the opposition in 1872 when Thiers was President. This was the most important change in the law of 1872 that was to occur during the Third Republic.

Although the Constitutional Law of 1875 made the only basic change in the law of 1872 on the Conseil d'Etat, there were a whole host of structural changes and adjustments in the number and qualifications of members during the Third Republic. In 1879 the republicans finally gained complete control of the Republic; MacMahon resigned on January 30 and Jules Grévy became President of the Republic. With MacMahon out of the way the republicans began in earnest their "purification" of the administration. On February 11th, the Vice-President of the Conseil d'Etat, Andral, was forced to resign; Faustin-Hélie, of republican sympathies, became the new Vice-President. Nine Councilors of State were dismissed and nine new Councilors of State were appointed to take their places.

The composition of the Conseil d'Etat was still further changed by the law of July 13, 1879. This law provided for a general increase in the membership of the Conseil; the number of Councilors of State was increased from twenty-two to thirty-two, the number of Maîtres des Requêtes from twenty-four to thirty, and the number of Auditors from thirty to thirty-six. Although the main purpose of the law was to give the Conseil a predominantly republican character, it incidentally gave the Conseil an addition of much-needed personnel. The work, especially the judicial work, of the Conseil had been increasing steadily since 1872. The committee, in 1872, had proposed a larger number of personnel, but because of the unsettled and adverse financial state of the country, the number had been reduced at the request of the chairman of the Finance Committee of the Assembly.

This was the last time during the Third Republic that the right of the executive to remove Councilors of State was exercised. It is clear from the debates in the National Assembly on the law of 1872 that the drafters of the law viewed the power of dismissal as a method to get rid of recalcitrant members. After 1879, owing in part to the increasing importance of its judicial function, the independence of the Conseil became a principle tacitly accepted by the government. Not until 1945 did the Conseil undergo another "purification" and then not even the irremovability of the ordinary judiciary prevented the government from dismissing judges. In spite of the power of the executive to remove Councilors of State, their security of tenure is, in effect, as great as that of irremovable judges. It is quite possible that the power would be used in the case of misconduct, but no such eventuality has ever arisen.

The law of 1879 further provided for the addition of a Section on Legislation to the Conseil and also abolished the examination for First Class Auditors. Henceforth First Class Auditors were merely appointed from Second Class Auditors by the President of the Republic on the recommendation of the Vice-President and the Section Presidents of the Conseil. The regulations governing the detached-service functions of members of the Conseil were also tightened by this law. A member was placed on detached service when he was called upon to occupy a post in the active administration. The name of the member on detached service was removed from the roster of the Conseil for the period he was away; when his detached service was completed, he was reinstated to the Conseil without loss of seniority when the first vacancy occurred. Some detached-service offices filled by members of the Conseil were ambassadorships, membership on international commissions and organizations, prefects, directors of ministerial departments, and advisory officials or governors-general in the colonies. Another office often filled by a member of the Conseil is that of cabinet chief (*chef du cabinet*) of a minister's cabinet. In this case the member of the Conseil, usually an Auditor, although the cabinet chief of the President of the Council is normally a Maître des Requêtes, is not detached officially and his name remains on the roster of the Conseil. The law of 1879 required that no one could be detached until he had served three years on the Conseil and then only for a period not exceeding three years without losing his rank on the roster. Nor could the number of members on detached service exceed 20 percent of the number of Councilors of State, Maîtres des Requêtes, or Auditors. This was an effective measure to prevent the depletion of the Conseil and thus hampering its work. Many of the members preferred being on detached service because, as a rule, salaries were higher,[44] but few would accept a detached-service office if it meant loss of seniority on the Conseil, for promotions were invariably based on seniority.

The Conseil, through its detached-service function, provided the government with a reservoir of highly trained administrators who could be called upon to perform important and highly diverse tasks. If the post was temporary, the government was relieved of finding another job for the administrator when the task was finished. Not only did the detached-service function offer this advantage to the government, but the Conseil also benefited; through these functions the members acquired valuable administrative experience which aided them in their work on the Conseil.

The section added to the Conseil d'Etat by the law of 1879, in spite of its being named the Section on Legislation, performed the same functions as the other administrative sections. Depending on which ministry a bill, regulation, decree, or request for advice came, the matter was deliberated and a report drafted in the section competent for that particular ministry.

Another modification of the law of 1872 occurred in 1880 when a law provided that Second Class Auditors would be paid after their first year's service on the Conseil. Shortly afterwards the first-year provision was dropped and Second Class Auditors were paid from the beginning of their service. These modifications increased the number of applicants who could hope to become Auditors. No longer was it necessary for the candidates to have independent means to support themselves during their first four years on the Conseil. The unpropertied classes continued to be effectively excluded, because to compete in the examinations one had to have a degree in law or its equivalent. After the basic diploma, the *baccalauréat*, it took three years to acquire the required degree. An education such as this required a considerable financial outlay, especially since the American custom of working one's way through college was unknown in France. After 1880, the Auditors came almost exclusively from the upper middle class.

Additional changes provided that Second Class Auditors could remain in that rank for a total of eight years. If, at the end of this period, they had not been appointed First Class Auditors, they were transferred to administrative posts outside the Conseil. After four years of service, an auditor could request such an appointment. The positions to which they could be appointed included: [45] (1) government commissioners [46] on the Council of Prefecture of the Seine, (2) secretary-general of a prefecture, either first or second class, (3) sub-prefects, first or second class, (4) substitute judge on a second class tribunal.

During the 1880's the judicial work of the Conseil continued to increase,[47] so much so that the additional work proved to be beyond the capacity of the Judicial Section. A considerable backlog of cases developed, which led, in 1888, to the creation of a temporary section [48] composed of a President of Section and four Councilors of State, one taken from each of the administrative sections. This temporary section was to relieve the Judicial Section of cases concerning taxation and elections. In 1900, further to expedite decisions, both the Judicial Section and the temporary Judicial Section were divided into two subsections; each subsection was capable of rendering definitive judgments.[49] Only important cases were carried to the whole section, or to the Public Assembly for judgment.

At the same time, the membership of the Conseil was slightly increased; there were to be forty Auditors and thirty-two Maîtres des Requêtes instead of thirty-six and thirty, respectively.[50] The additional members were assigned to the two judicial sections, which were being deluged by the number of cases brought before the Conseil. The splitting of the two sections into four subsections, each capable of final decision, doubled the organs of judgment. This reform required only a slight addition of personnel and did not materially affect the standard of justice. Henceforth, the whole section was not required to sit on minor cases which by their nature did not require a full section. The judgment of these minor cases was generally a routine matter once the facts were known and evaluated.

The reform law of 1900 also provided that at least two thirds of the Maîtres des Requêtes were to be appointed from First Class Auditors,[51] instead of one third as required by the law of 1872. A new feature was included to the effect that at least one half of the Councilors of State had to be named from Maîtres des

Requêtes. These proportions were increased by laws passed in 1910 and 1923: three fourths of the Maîtres des Requêtes had to be appointed from First Class Auditors and two thirds of the Councilors of State had to be appointed from among Maîtres des Requêtes.[52] The reason for these changes was that too many persons, without proper experience, were being appointed from the outside. For example, a departing minister, who desired to find a position for his cabinet chief, would get him appointed as a Maître des Requêtes.[53]

The criticism that such appointments as these aroused led to the adoption of the above mentioned restrictions, and these restrictions were further tightened by the finance law of 1911. This law provided that to be appointed a Maître des Requêtes one must have served in the administration at least ten years;[54] the minimum age for Maîtres des Requêtes was raised to thirty and that of Councilors of State to forty. The effect of these restrictions was to limit "political" appointments.

In 1910, after twenty-two years of operation, the temporary Judicial Section was made into a permanent section. The organs of judgment in the two judicial sections were further multiplied to three subsections in each judicial section. This change was another reflection of the increasing number of cases brought before the Conseil d'Etat. In succeeding years the number of cases was to increase still more.

The first month of the First World War saw the departure of almost all the Auditors and Maîtres des Requêtes to military service. No one thought that the war would last very long, and though the more immediate work of the Conseil was kept up to date by its elder members, the judicial work was permitted to accumulate. In 1913, the judicial sections judged 4,190 cases as compared to only 895 for 1915.[55] Between 1910 and 1915, the backlog of cases to be judged remained at approximately six thousand. Since during this period the rate of judgment was slightly over four thousand a year, the Conseil was about a year and a half behind in its work. In 1917 the number of cases unjudged had increased to 7,125, but by 1919 this figure had dropped to 5,664.[56] This decline was only temporary, however, because an additional influx of cases arising directly from the war came after 1919.

The slowness of judgment was quite a problem then, and still is. There were examples of petitions registered in 1913 and 1914 which were not judged until 1922 and in some cases this delay amounted to a virtual denial of justice. For example, there is the case of a petition registered in 1913 by a parent contesting the legality of the establishment of a coeducational school. In this case the decision was not rendered until 1922, after the child had finished his schooling.[57] The delay between the registration of a case and its judgment was disadvantageous to the State as well as to individuals. In cases where the State was condemned for damages, it could be condemned to pay interest on the sum; from 1909 to 1914, the State paid 230,730 francs in interest alone.[58] Clearly some reform to speed up the judgment of cases was necessary.

Two types of reform were considered: one was simply to augment the personnel and to increase the number of subsections in order to meet the increasing judicial work of the Conseil; the other was to decrease the jurisdiction of the Conseil either by making the Councils of Prefecture, or an analogous creation, the judge of last resort for certain types of less important cases,[59] or by decreasing the jurisdiction of the Conseil in favor of the ordinary judicial courts. There was general resistance to allowing the Councils of Prefecture to judge cases in last resort, no matter how minor. The personnel of the Councils of Prefecture generally had little technical competence and were always inclined to judge in favor of the government. Also, they were too easily influenced by the prefect. As Professor Laferrière remarked in 1920:

It is generally acknowledged that the Councils of Prefecture do not afford sufficient guarantees that the judgment of cases in last resort, no matter how unimportant, can be assigned to them. The jurisdiction of the Councils of Prefecture is tolerated, in spite of its known imperfections, precisely because of the possibility to appeal any case to the Conseil d'Etat.[60]

For this reason it was proposed, by those who wished to diminish the jurisdiction of the Conseil d'Etat in favor of a lower jurisdiction, to replace the Councils of Prefecture by establishing a small number of regional councils with a method of recruiting personnel akin to the Conseil d'Etat.[61] There was little support of the plan to give the ordinary judicial courts jurisdiction over certain types of cases.[62]

The government adopted the former alternative, that of increasing the personnel and multiplying the subsections. On December 23, 1919, the Minister of Justice, Louis Nail, presented a bill to the Chamber for the reform of the Conseil d'Etat; this bill proposed to increase the subsections in each judicial section to five and to increase the number of Councilors from thirty-five to forty-two, the Maîtres des Requêtes from thirty-seven to forty-three, and the Auditors from forty to forty-eight. The bill was sent to the Committee on Civil and Criminal Legislation of the Chamber, which reported it on June 4, 1920, with only minor amendments. The Chamber voted the text on July 29 without any debate. The Senate committee adopted the bill voted by the Chamber with two minor amendments. But the Senate, in an economy mood, did not desire to create any new posts and voted (126-123) to send the bill back to the committee, and there it stayed.

Another bill, proposed by Louis Marin in the Chamber, which never got further than the committee, proposed a more radical reform of the Conseil. The Marin bill proposed the establishment of regional councils to replace the Councils of Prefecture and they were to be given final jurisdiction over cases concerning taxation and pensions. Of the annual average of some four thousand cases judged by the Conseil d'Etat before 1914, Marin considered only about five hundred important enough to be judged by the Conseil d'Etat.[63] He proposed to add a corporative representation to the Conseil, representing the liberal professions, unions, employers, agriculture, commerce, etc. In this way Marin hoped to increase the technical competence of the Conseil so as to better enable it to fulfill its task as technical counselor of the government.

None of these bills ended in legislation. However, to relieve the Conseil of some of the cases arising directly out of the war, special jurisdictions were set up to hear cases on war-damage reparation and military pensions, with the Conseil d'Etat only hearing appeals in cassation. During this period quasi-judicial councils were created in various ministries, as for example in the Ministry of Labor, where a quasi-judicial council was created to hear petitions concerning social security. Although appeal was possible to the Conseil d'Etat, most of the claimants were satisfied that the law had been applied fairly and did not appeal.

Because of the determination of the Senate to create no new posts, a new minister of justice, Louis Barthou, presented a bill which avoided increasing the personnel; it finally passed the Senate on January 23, 1923. The Chamber voted the bill without debate, at the request of Maurice Colrat, Barthou's successor, on March 1, 1923. The law provided for an increase to six subsections in one of the judicial sections but left the other as before. The judicial personnel of the Conseil was also augmented by taking one Councilor of State from each of the administrative sections. The law was only a palliative, and not an effective one at that.

In 1926 the government took an important step in overhauling the administrative jurisdiction by reforming the Councils of Prefecture. Before 1926 there had been a Council of Prefecture in each department, but the decree-law of September 6, 1926, consolidated the Councils of Prefecture to form twenty-two Interdepartmental Councils of Prefecture, except for the Council of Prefecture of the Seine, which was left intact owing to its heavy burden. The jurisdiction of these Councils was increased by the decree-law of May 5, 1934, for departmental and communal matters concerning actions in responsibility, contracts, and the civil service law. These laws diminished the administrative functions of the Councils and raised the qualifications for appointment to them. In effect, these reforms recognized that the Interdepartmental Councils of Prefecture were primarily judicial bodies and gave them jurisdiction over certain types of cases formerly judged by the Conseil d'Etat.

During the 1930's parliament resorted again to increasing the personnel and the number of subsections in an effort to relieve the overcrowded docket. The membership of the Conseil was increased in 1930; although the number of personnel was reduced in 1934 as an economy measure, these cuts were restored in 1937.[64] In 1933, the number of subsections in both of the judicial sections was raised to six. These measures, like others taken since the end of the First World War, had not been effective in relieving the overcrowded docket by the time the Conseil entered the troubled period of the Second World War.

3

THE STRUCTURE OF THE CONSEIL D'ETAT SINCE 1940

THE defeat of the French in June, 1940, caused a drastic shake-up in France's constitutional structure. General de Gaulle, the former undersecretary of war, went to London and formed a "Free French" government, while at home the legislative assemblies voted to delegate their power to Marshal Pétain.

VICHY AND FREE FRANCE (1940–45)

The effect of the defeat on the Conseil d'Etat was slight; the Vichy government retained the Conseil almost exactly as it had been under the Third Republic. The law of December 18, 1940, which was the basic statute of the Conseil under the Vichy regime, was merely a codification of the various legal texts that were in effect at the end of the Third Republic. Even though the basic structure of the Conseil remained substantially the same, the defeat brought about other changes. The Conseil, now deprived of its home in the Palais Royal in Paris owing to the German occupation, found refuge at Royat, a watering-place near Vichy. The members of the Conseil, like all other civil servants, were required to take a personal oath of allegiance to Marshal Pétain. Approximately 8 percent of the members of the Conseil were removed owing to the Vichy racial laws and a few members took refuge outside France, but aside from these changes the Vichy Conseil d'Etat had the same personnel as did the Conseil in 1939.

The functions of the Conseil were much the same, though the absence of an elected assembly brought about an increase in the function of technical counselor. The Vichy government submitted the majority of its proposed laws to the examination of the Conseil d'Etat, which was a departure from the practice of the Third Republic. The Conseil was relatively docile, though in its judicial capacity it mitigated by strict interpretation the application of some of the Vichy laws, such as the racial laws, the corporative laws, and statutes governing civil servants.[1] The Conseil strictly interpreted the racial laws so as to exclude many people who might have been affected by them. The Conseil did not attempt to contravene the literal provisions of Vichy laws as contrary to the constitution or the general principles of French public law. Since the Revolution of 1789, no jurisdiction in France has ever passed on the constitutionality of legislative acts.[2]

In London, in addition to the National Committee, de Gaulle's advisory and legislative body, there was set up a Commission on Legislation, at first composed almost entirely of former judges, civil servants, and professors, to whom were later added former parliamentarians. This Commission prepared, or changed into correct legal form, all proposed ordinances.[3] The term "ordinance" as equivalent to law (*loi*) was employed because law, in its strict sense, refers specifically to an enactment of an elected assembly. By not using the term "law," the de Gaulle government showed its respect for parliamentary legality, a necessary step owing to its claim that the Vichy regime was illegal. The monarchical term "ordinance" had not been used since the July Monarchy. After the liberation of France, ordinances were recognized as part of the law of the land. The ordinances of the Free French and provisional governments are as much a part of French legislation today as the laws enacted under the Third Republic and the unrepealed Vichy "laws."

The Judicial Commission, another body set up by the London Government, operated in judicial matters as a Conseil d'Etat. Its effective jurisdiction included those colonies which had adhered to the Free French cause. When the government was transferred to Algiers, the Commission became the Temporary Judicial Committee and functioned as an administrative law court until August of 1944, when the metropolitan Conseil d'Etat was again available.

When the London National Committee was transformed into the French Committee of National Liberation at Algiers, the Committee on Legislation became the Juridical Committee. Established by the ordinance of August 6, 1943, the Juridical Committee was composed of ten members under the presidency of René Cassin, a former professor of law at the University of Paris, who had been de Gaulle's legal advisor in London. It was charged with three main functions: (1) to give advice in place of the Conseil d'Etat in all cases where legislation anterior to 1940 obliged the government to ask the advice of the Conseil, (2) to study the revision of laws and regulations of public administration preparatory to the transfer of the provisional government to France, (3) to put into legal form all proposed ordinances, making the text clear, coherent, and consistent with other legislation. Of these three tasks the first was dropped in October 1944 after the Conseil d'Etat became available. It continued to perform the other two functions until July 31, 1945, when it became a part of the Conseil d'Etat known as the Permanent Commission.

The post-liberation purge of members of the Conseil, who were thought to have been too much in sympathy with the Vichy regime, was more extensive than in 1879. It affected about 20 percent of the total membership. Alfred Porché, the Vice-President of the Conseil was one of those removed;[4] he was replaced as Vice-President by René Cassin. In the "purification" three devices were employed: dismissal, retirement (on pension), and as a lighter form of punishment suspension (*mise en disponibilité*) for a period, usually three years. The two incidents of mass removals, and in fact the only examples of the removal of members of the Conseil, 1879 and 1945, came in important periods of change, the former when the republicans captured the Republic and the latter at the fall of the Vichy regime. These removals cannot be considered as derogations of the principle of independence of the membership of the Conseil. In 1945, not even the irremovable members of the regular judiciary escaped.

In the latter part of 1944, a Commission was formed, under the presidency of René Cassin, to draw up a proposed ordinance for the reform of the Conseil d'Etat. The Commission was composed of members of the Conseil and representatives of the various resistance groups. The recommendations of the Commission were embodied in a report made in the name of the Commission by Henry Puget to the minister of justice. The Commission proposed changes along the following lines:

> In sum, the present moment appears to require: an extension of the attributions and activity of the Conseil—a tightening of the connections with the central organism of the government, while at the same time preserving the rhythm of work; an increase in the competence of members in various fields and improvement of their communication with the administrative services; [and] finally, an amelioration of the conditions of access to the competitive examination in favor of young people of talent and character, however modest their social origins. It is along these lines that the Commission has principally oriented its effort.[5]

The Commission proposed to bring the Conseil closer to the President of the Council of Ministers and to make it more convenient for the Council of Ministers to utilize the Conseil:

> Outside and above the ministerial bureaus and the consultative councils, it is necessary for the men in power to be able to inform themselves from a corps [the Conseil d'Etat] with general competence, uniting great knowledge with continuous experience, close enough to the operation of the administration to know its needs and functions, yet far enough removed from the ministries and special interests to be able to examine questions in their entirety and to discern the solutions conforming most to the public good and to law.[6]

The Commission held that the union of the executive and legislative powers in the provisional government made the consultation of the Conseil on ordinances and decrees all the more desirable.

To insure this collaboration between the government and the Conseil d'Etat, the Commission proposed that the functions of the Juridical Committee be transferred to the Conseil d'Etat. Thus, all proposed ordinances would have to be submitted to the Conseil d'Etat. Proposed ordinances or bills that were declared urgent would be examined by a new body created in the Conseil, the Permanent Commission. Other bills would, as before, be examined by the competent administrative section for the ministry from which the bill emanated, and afterward by the General Assembly. The Secretariat of the President of the Council of Ministers alone would be able to declare bills urgent. A Maître des Requêtes would be assigned to the secretariat of the President of the Council of Ministers to provide a liaison and take care of the affairs interesting the Conseil.

The Commission proposed that three members of the Conseil be assigned to inspect the subordinate administrative jurisdictions in metropolitan France and the overseas territories. This innovation was adopted in the final ordinance but the proposal to call the effective head of the Conseil the President, instead of the Vice-President, was not.

During the Third Republic, the title of Councilor of State in special service (*en service extraordinaire*) was given to directors and secretaries-general of the ministries. However, these titularies rarely attended the meetings of the section or the General Assembly. Because the title of Councilor of State in special service had become almost purely honorific and its holders remained generally unknown,[7] the Commission proposed to reduce the number to twelve, these to be chosen outside the administration. The new Councilors of State in special service were to be named from persons who had achieved renown in various fields of activity, such as commerce, industry, labor unions, agriculture, etc. This recommendation for a corporate representation on the Conseil is reminiscent of the bill proposed by Louis Marin in the early twenties, but its application by the Commission was on a much smaller scale. These members were to be invited by the

Vice-President to participate in all matters of which they had a special knowledge and were to be given a vote only on these matters. The proposals of the Commission in this regard were embodied in the ordinance of July 31, 1945. Appointments were to last for a year, though the Commission had originally proposed a three-year term.

Although deprived of the title of Councilors of State in special service, the directors and secretaries-general were to have the right to defend the bills of their ministries before the different echelons of the Conseil. They were to have the title of Government Commissioners [8] and the right to vote on the various matters concerning their ministry. These suggestions by the Commission were incorporated into the ordinance as it was finally adopted.

In an attempt to cement relations between the Conseil and the active administration, the Commission wished to institute a new category of Maîtres des Requêtes in temporary service. They were to be appointed from the administration and to stay on the Conseil for three years, at the end of which time they would return to the administration. These appointees would become familiar with the work of the Conseil, which would benefit from their administrative experience. After their departure, they would carry back to the administration a respect for the work of the Conseil.[9] One of the main reasons for this provision was to permit members of the Councils of Prefecture to spend three years on the Conseil absorbing administrative jurisprudence, thus making them better qualified as judges after their return to the Councils of Prefecture. This suggestion was not embodied in the final ordinance.

As has been said above, the Commission wished to make the auditorship more accessible, especially to youths from the lower-income groups. Unlike the Third Republic, the Fourth was to have "careers open to talent." In 1936 a bulletin of the *Ecole libre des sciences politiques* announced that of 124 Auditors received into the Conseil d'Etat since 1900, 121 had attended the *Ecole libre*.[10] The report of the Commission recognized this:

In fact, preparation takes place exclusively at the *Ecole libre des sciences politiques*. The celebrated institution of the rue St. Guillaume has possessed for a long time a sort of monopoly of access to the important corps of the state. Its instruction corresponds to the program of examinations. It is only in its courses that certain matters are sufficiently studied. It alone has instituted lectures especially oriented to the end to be attained.[11]

The *Ecole libre* was a private institution and although fees were not high, students usually had to have some private means. Only twenty scholarships existed for the whole school. The Commission argued that this monopoly was open to criticism, considering the staid and conservative spirit of the institution.[12]

When the report of the Commission was drafted the proposal for a school of administration run by the government was as yet unrealized. The Commission proposed that the Conseil d'Etat itself open a special school, accessible to all, to prepare students for the Auditors' examination; the teaching would be undertaken by members of the Conseil. This special school never came into being, mainly because the proposed *Ecole nationale d'administration* was created in the meantime. Nevertheless, it illustrates the desire of the Commission to "enlarge the base of recruitment in a democratic spirit." [13]

The only change proposed by the Commission regarding the judicial work of the Conseil was in regard to automobile accidents. During the Third Republic accidents in which a vehicle of the civil service was involved could give rise to a petition of the Conseil d'Etat for damages. The number of such cases increased proportionately with vehicular traffic. The Commission wished to make the ordinary courts competent for such accidents, relieving the Conseil of a large number of cases which were usually of minor importance. This suggestion was not, however, incorporated into the ordinance. Thus, the main innovations proposed by the Commission were: (1) all government bills were to be submitted to the Conseil, (2) certain features were designed to insure a closer relation with the cabinet, (3) the recruitment of Auditors was to be more democratic.

THE FOURTH REPUBLIC AND AFTER

As has been indicated above, the recommendations of the Commission were, in the main, accepted and were embodied in the ordinance of July 31, 1945. This law is now the basic statute on the Conseil d'Etat, as the law of May 24, 1872, was for the Conseil during the Third Republic. Whereas the law of May 24, 1872, was a product of three parliamentary readings, which gave rise to heated debate, the 1945 ordinance, by contrast, came into existence almost unnoticed. The proposed ordinance was submitted to the Conseil d'Etat for advice, adopted by the French Committee of National Liberation, and promulgated by the provisional government of General de Gaulle.

The ordinance increased the membership of the Conseil by about 10 percent over the Third Republic and Vichy levels; it provided for one Vice-President, five Section Presidents, forty-two Councilors of State in ordinary service, forty-five Maîtres des Requêtes, twenty First Class Auditors, and twenty-four Second Class Auditors. As before, at least two thirds of the Councilors of State were to be chosen from Maîtres de Requêtes and at least three fourths of the Maîtres des Requêtes from First Class Auditors; all First Class Auditors were to be chosen from Second Class Auditors. It was provided that if an Auditor showed himself to be incapable or unfit, he could be transferred from the Conseil to another post in the public service. However, this has never been done.

Instead of being selected directly by means of a competitive examination conducted by the Conseil d'Etat as formerly, the Auditors now come from the *Ecole nationale d'administration*. This school combines the recruiting for the "three great corps"

(The Conseil d'Etat, the Inspection of Finance, and the Court of Accounts) as well as for the diplomatic service and prefectural corps, and other posts in various ministries. Every year a class of students is selected by competitive examination for the three-year training program of the school. Those qualifying have usually had some training at a Faculty of Law, the *Institut d'études politiques* in Paris (formerly the *Ecole libre*), or one of the *Institut d'études politiques* around the country. The *Ecole nationale d'administration* is especially geared to give the students specialized training fitting them for the public service, as formerly did the *Ecole libre des sciences politiques*. A large part of the instruction at the *Ecole nationale d'administration* is given by high-ranking public servants, among whom are several members of the Conseil d'Etat. At the end of the three years the first twenty-five or so of the students, by order of their academic rank in the class, can choose the corps to which they wish to belong, dependent of course on the number of vacancies. A student finishing twenty-fifth may be forced to choose the Court of Accounts because the vacancies on the Conseil d'Etat and the Inspection of Finance may have been filled by students ranked before him. The rest of the students find employment in various ministries or in the Councils of Prefecture, now called Administrative Tribunals. Under this system the Conseil d'Etat has always received a large share of the best students. For example, in 1952, with seven vacancies in the auditorship, the students finishing second, fourth, fifth, twelfth, thirteenth, fourteenth, and fifteenth chose the Conseil d'Etat. The other eight of the first fifteen chose the Inspection of Finance and of those choosing the Court of Accounts, the highest ranking was sixteenth.[14]

There were seventy-four graduates of the *Ecole d'administration* in the class of 1952, and one third of them were able to choose one of the important corps. These seventy-four were all that remained of some 1,200 candidates who had taken the entrance examination in 1948.[15] A comparison of these figures with the number who took the examination for Second Class Auditor during the Third Republic illustrates not so much a greater interest in entering the public service among the young as an increased accessibility to the higher branches of the public service. There were two women among the seven Auditors recruited by the Conseil in 1952, which marked the first time that women have ever become Auditors since the foundation of the Conseil in 1800. This method of choosing Second Class Auditors has the disadvantage that some who choose the Conseil d'Etat might have preferred another corps.[16] For this reason some of the older members of the Conseil would prefer to return to the system used under the Third Republic.

The ordinance of 1945 provided for five sections in the Conseil, of which four are administrative and one judicial; the four administrative sections are the Section of Interior, the Section of Finance, the Section of Public Works, and the Social Section. A regulation of public administration of July 30, 1945, provided that matters originating in the following ministries should resort to the following sections—*Section of Interior:* from the Ministries of Justice, Interior, National Education, and Information; *Section of Finance:* from the Ministries of Finance, Foreign Affairs, War, Navy, Air, and Colonies; *Section of Public Works:* from the Ministries of National Economy, Public Works and Transportation, Industrial Production, Agriculture, Food, Post-Telephone-Telegraph, Reconstruction and Urbanism; *Social Section:* from the Ministries of Labor, Social Security, Public Health, Prisoners of War and Deportees and Refugees.

Each administrative section is composed of a Section President and six Councilors of State plus an indefinite number of Maîtres des Requêtes and Auditors, varying from section to section.

Matters interesting more than one ministry, for which two different administrative sections are competent, are examined by the sections meeting together. All bills except those declared "urgent," which go to the Permanent Commission, regulations of public administration, and many enumerated matters such as

STRUCTURE OF THE CONSEIL SINCE 1940

the creation of religious establishments, certain contracts passed by the City of Paris, and boundary changes of communes are submitted to the General Assembly after they have been examined by the appropriate section. Technically all the personnel of the Conseil d'Etat as well as the Councilors of State in special service and the ministers are members of the General Assembly.

The President of the Council of Ministers is the titular presiding officer of the General Assembly, although he rarely presides.[17] In the absence of the President of the Council, the presiding officer is the minister of justice, who in fact never presides over the Conseil more than once during the life of any cabinet, and many times not at all. Normally the Vice-President of the Conseil d'Etat presides over the General Assembly. All Councilors in ordinary service and Councilors in special service can vote in the General Assembly; ministers can vote only on affairs involving their ministry. The reporter of the matter also has the right to vote. All others have the right to express their opinions. In any matter, of the members allowed to vote, the regular members of the Conseil are always in the majority. The General Assembly cannot deliberate unless more than twenty Councilors of State and Presidents of Section are present.

The Judicial Section comprises a Section President, an Assistant President,[18] about half of the total number of Councilors of State, and more than half of the total number of Maîtres des Requêtes and auditors. The Judicial Section is divided into eleven subsections numbered one to eleven, not all of which have the same powers.[19] Six of the subsections meet separately for the preparation of reports and discussion, but for the judgment of a case, two of them unite to form one unit. The other five subsections are independent organs of judgment; these subsections judge less important cases, such as those involving pensions, elections, taxes, requisitions, and indemnities for motor-vehicle accidents. On thorny or delicate matters, however, two of these subsections can unite for judgment. Each subsection has a presiding officer chosen from among the Councilors of State, not upon the basis of seniority but on the basis of capability. When two subsections unite for judgment the oldest subsection president in point of service in that position presides. For a subsection to make a decision, three members having the right to vote must be present, two of whom must be Councilors of State; for two subsections united the number is five. In case an even number of members are present and the vote ends in a tie, a supplementary member is usually brought in to break the tie. A decision rendered by any organ of judgment—a subsection, two subsections united, the whole Judicial Section, or the Plenary Assembly—has the same weight.

Important cases are carried to the full Judicial Section. This section is composed of all the presiding officers of all the eleven subsections, plus two members of the subsection(s) where the report on the case under discussion was prepared. Either the Vice-President of the Conseil or the President of the Judicial Section presides over this section.

The highest organ of judgment is the Plenary Assembly, formerly called the Public Assembly, which judges only cases of the highest importance. It is composed of the Vice-President, who presides, the President of the Judicial Section, the presiding officers of all the subsections, and four other Councilors of State, one from each of the administrative sections elected each year by the General Assembly. The accompanying diagram shows the organs of judgment of the Conseil d'Etat in judicial matters. There are twelve organs of judgment.

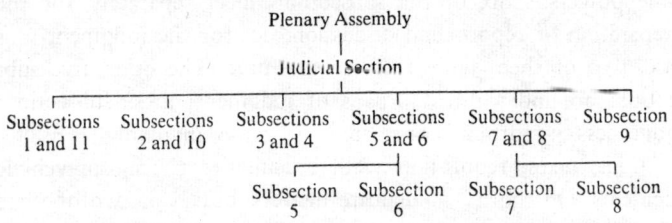

ORGANS OF JUDGMENT FOR JUDICIAL MATTERS

STRUCTURE OF THE CONSEIL SINCE 1940

The appointment to the higher ranks of the Conseil is in the hands of the government. The Vice-President of the Conseil d'Etat is chosen from among the Section Presidents or from among the Councilors of State, on the recommendation of the minister of justice, by a decree in the Council of Ministers. The Section Presidents are chosen in the same manner, from among the Councilors of State. Councilors of State are also chosen by a decree in the Council of Ministers on the recommendation of the minister of justice. In the case of the two thirds who must be chosen from among the Maîtres des Requêtes, the Vice-President, after consulting the Section Presidents, submits the nominations; three names are submitted, usually in the order of seniority of Maîtres des Requêtes and the government chooses from these three. The top name submitted is usually the one to receive the appointment. It is possible for either the Vice-President or the government to prevent the promotion of a Maître des Requêtes, but examples of this are rare.[20]

Maîtres des Requêtes and First Class Auditors are named by decrees of the minister of justice. In the case of Maîtres des Requêtes, of those chosen from among First Class Auditors, as three fourths must be, the Vice-President after consulting the Section Presidents makes the recommendations to the minister of justice. In practice three names are submitted, again usually in order of seniority. First Class Auditors are selected in the same manner, all from among Second Class Auditors. Second Class Auditors are recruited, as described above, from the *Ecole nationale d'administration*.

There are several age and service requirements: Councilors of State must be at least forty years old; Maîtres des Requêtes appointed from outside the Conseil must be at least thirty and have served in the civil or the military service for ten years. The ten-year service provision is to prevent abuse in appointments of personnel drawn from outside the Conseil.

The Vice-President, the Section Presidents, and Councilors of State can be dismissed by a decree in the Council of Ministers, on the proposal of the minister of justice. The Maîtres des Requêtes and Auditors can be dismissed on the advice of the Vice-President, after consulting the Section Presidents, by a decree of the minister of justice.[21] Dismissal, as has been said before, is an extraordinary procedure. Since 1872 the only examples of the dismissal of Councilors of State occurred in 1879 and 1945. However, the government has yet another weapon which it used in 1879 and 1945, that of retiring members on their pension. The normal retirement age for the Vice-President and Councilors of State is seventy.[22] Members can be retired before attaining this age by a decree in the Council of Ministers on the proposal of the minister of justice. The employment of this device is rare and, as has been pointed out above, has occurred only in times of sweeping governmental changes. Aside from these exceptions, the members of the Conseil are generally free from governmental pressure. As a court, the Conseil is completely independent, in fact probably freer from pressure than the ordinary judiciary, where advancement is not necessarily based on seniority.[23]

The independence of the Conseil was a development which took place in the early years of the Third Republic. The sentiment during the debates on the law of 1872 was that the government would exercise its power of dismissal freely, especially with regard to the nonjudicial membership. The matter was complicated in the early years of the Third Republic when the Assembly, out of enmity for Thiers, retained the right to appoint and dismiss Councilors itself. In 1872, Dufaure pointed out that dismissal by the Assembly would be very difficult. This is proof that the government considered dismissal as a weapon which would be used to insure the subservience of the Conseil. After the resignation of Thiers, as has been discussed above, the power of appointment and dismissal was returned to the executive. And after the fall of MacMahon, when the republicans captured the Republic, the weapon was actually used for the first and last time during the Third Republic. After 1879, the independence of the members of the Conseil came to be accepted. The growth of the principle of independence was aided by the increasing importance of the Conseil as a judicial body and any governmental attempt at dismissal would have run the risk of arousing adverse public opinion.

The problem of an overloaded docket is one which has been plaguing the Conseil since 1910. The result has been that petitioners have had to wait from two to five years, or sometimes even longer, before their cases are decided. Two solutions have been regularly applied to this situation since 1872: (1) an increase in the personnel devoted to the judicial work of the Conseil; (2) an increase in the number of subsections which are competent to judge cases. Both of these solutions have about outlived their usefulness: to increase the membership of the Conseil further would have the effect of making it too large and unwieldy and in addition might destroy its unique corporate spirit. To increase the number of subsections would have the effect of lowering the high judicial standards of the Conseil; this type of reform would reduce the number of personnel in the existing subsections, thereby increasing the burden of work on each member.

A solution suggested several times after the First World War was revived in 1948 by the Vice-President of the Conseil d'Etat. In the second number of *Etudes et documents,* an annual publication of the Conseil, Vice-President René Cassin signalized the need for reform. He pointed out that of the regular judicial matters (*grand contentieux*), as opposed to the less exacting cases involving elections, direct taxes, and pensions (*petit contentieux*), the Conseil in the judicial year 1938–39 [24] received 1,931 cases. For the same type of regular judicial matters in the year 1945–46, the Conseil received 4,963 cases and in the year 1946–47, 5,410.[25] This was a remarkable increase. In the postwar period the Conseil has registered more than two and one half times as many cases per twelve-month period as in 1938–39. The backlog of unjudged cases (*grand contentieux* only) was 2,799 on August 1, 1939, and 10,465 on August 1, 1947.[26] After 1947, the backlog continued to increase. For the judicial year 1946–47, 6,772 cases of all types were registered. For the same period the Conseil rendered 4,308 decisions. Thus the backlog, in a single year, was increased by almost 2,500 cases.

To remedy this situation, the Vice-President proposed that the Interdepartmental Councils of Prefecture be made the judges in first instance in the administrative jurisdiction, with the exception of pleas of *ultra vires* (*recours d'annulation pour excès de pouvoir*) directed against the central authorities, for which the Conseil would remain the judge of first and last resort.[27] The Conseil, of course, would remain a court of appeal from the Councils of Prefecture. In effect, this type of reform would relieve the Conseil of original jurisdiction for the majority of *ultra vires* cases; only those petitions directed against the central authorities were to come to the Conseil in first instance. Since the law of 1926, which replaced the departmental Councils of Prefecture by Interdepartmental Councils of Prefecture, the quality of these Councils had improved. The Vice-President noted:

It [the reform] is possible immediately, because the present Interdepartmental Councils of Prefecture are not actually overworked, nor all sufficiently occupied. The very small percentage of decisions annulled in appeal by the Conseil d'Etat already constitutes a guarantee of the general quality of the decisions of these Councils.[28]

How different this comment is from the comments on the Councils of Prefecture voiced during the debates on the law of 1872. In addition, since 1945 the Conseil d'Etat has had a permanent mission of inspection over the Councils of Prefecture. This inspection was supposed particularly to keep the Councils informed of the latest trends in the jurisprudence of the Conseil and to suggest means to improve the standards of these bodies. The reform proposed by Vice-President Cassin would have the advantage of entailing no additional financial outlay.

In spite of this advantage it was not until June 15, 1950, that the government introduced a bill to reform the Conseil in the sense proposed by the Vice-President. Like all bills emanating from the government, this bill was submitted to the Conseil d'Etat for advice, and it was approved by the Conseil. The bill was also approved by the Committee on the Judiciary of the Assembly but no action was taken on it until March, 1953, when it was placed on the parliamentary calendar by the Mayer government. Meanwhile the backlog of cases before the Conseil was increasing yearly. On August 1, 1952, it stood at 23,390.[29] The effectiveness of the judicial work of the Conseil had been endangered.

The debates on the bill began on March 13 and continued on March 19 and 26.[30] However, the fall of the Mayer government on May 21 found the bill only in its second reading. There the matter rested until the law of July 11, 1953, which granted the government, for a limited time, special decree powers in financial and administrative matters. Article 7 of the law of July 11, 1953, provided that the government could decree "the reform of administrative adjudication which must be completed before October 1, 1953."

Two decrees of September 30, 1953,[31] issued under Article 7 of the law of July 11, 1953, enacted, with a few minor modifications, the text which the Assembly had examined. The Interdepartmental Councils of Prefecture were renamed "Administrative Tribunals," [32] to emphasize the fact that they were courts and not subsidiaries of the Prefect. The Administrative Tribunals were given original jurisdiction in administrative cases, except for certain pleas of *ultra vires* directed against the central government and cases overlapping the jurisdiction of a single Tribunal.[33] The qualifications for membership on the Tribunals were raised. In order to make the positions more desirable, three new members were added to the Conseil d'Etat, one Councilor of State and two Maîtres de Requêtes, to be reserved for the members of the Administrative Tribunals.[34]

This reform was intended to lighten the load on the docket of the Conseil d'Etat and decrease the amount of time between the registration of a petition and its judgment. Although the decisions of the Administrative Tribunals might be appealed to the Conseil, it was hoped that only a small part would be. In order to further lighten the overcrowded docket of the Conseil, all cases which would come under the competence of the Administrative Tribunals were reassigned to these courts, unless the Conseil had already taken steps toward the judgment of these cases. Thus, some 8,500 cases were reassigned to the Administrative Tribunals.[35]

By August 1, 1958, it was apparent that the reform had been partially successful. The number of pending cases before the Conseil had been reduced to approximately 10,000. This reduction from a high of more than 26,000, which existed at the end of 1953, was owing to two reasons: first, the transfer of some 8,500 cases to the Administrative Tribunals, and second, the reduction in the number of cases registered on the docket of the Conseil after the reform. The Conseil has been able to judge more cases than have been registered since 1954. For example, during the judicial year 1957–58, the Conseil rendered 4,959 decisions and 3,104 new cases were registered. Thus during the year the backlog was reduced by 1,855 cases. To the great benefit of petitioners, the delay in judgment has been cut approximately in half since the 1953 reform.

THE SPIRIT OF THE CONSEIL D'ETAT

Before moving on to the following chapters, which will deal with the legislative, administrative, and judicial work of the Conseil, something should be said of the procedural method employed by the Conseil and the spirit which permeates this institution. There are forms of procedure that are not covered by the laws and regulations governing the Conseil. Certain procedures are the result of tradition, others of common sense. Nor is the action of individuals in any institution of this sort purely negligible.

The most important single member of the Conseil is the Vice-

President. He is in charge of the administration of the Conseil and if he is a particularly strong individual, he can, within limits, give the Conseil a general orientation. The Vice-President is responsible for the conduct of the Conseil's members and in some measure controls their careers. It is the Vice-President who, after consulting the Presidents of Section, recommends members to the minister of justice for promotion. Moreover, the Vice-President has a great deal to say in the assignment of personnel to the various sections of the Conseil. Before members of the Conseil are placed on detached service in order to occupy positions in the administration, the advice of the Vice-President and the Section Presidents is solicited by the government.

The Vice-President presides over the debates of the General Assembly and the Plenary Assembly (formerly the Public Assembly). These two assemblies deal with the most important matters which come to the Conseil, the former for legislative and administrative matters and the latter for judicial matters. The Vice-President, if he desires, can preside over any of the units of the Conseil. Some Vice-Presidents have utilized this power to give the work of a section, or a special commission, an orientation conforming to their views.[36] For example, the government entrusted the Conseil d'Etat with preparing the bill which finally became the Law of Associations of 1901. Georges Coulon, then the Vice-President, created a special commission for the task and presided over it himself. He also personally directed the preparation of the regulations of public administration which provided for the execution of the law of 1905 on the separation of Church and State.[37] Coulon was a strong laic and an economic liberal.

His influence was felt on all the regulations that the Conseil d'Etat was called upon to prepare or examine, be they for the *défense républicaine*, the application of financial policy and customs legislation, the development of social reforms, the extension of the rights of labor unions, or the drafting of military laws.[38]

Even more important was the work of Coulon's predecessor, Edouard Laferrière, who presided over the Conseil for sixteen years. Laferrière was the prime mover in extending the jurisdiction of the Conseil and developing the plea of *ultra vires* to the position of importance which it holds today. In 1886, while Vice-President, Laferrière published the first volume of his famous *Traité de la juridiction administrative et de recours contentieux*. This work was the first synthesis of the rules applied in administrative law by the Conseil d'Etat; it formed a solid foundation for the jurisprudence of the Conseil and a point of departure for further development. Another great jurist, Gaston Jèze, has characterized administrative law before Laferrière as "chaotic." [39]

The Vice-President also represents the Conseil in its relations with the President of the Council and the minister of justice, either of whom may ask for his assistance. Problems which arise in the work of the Conseil often lead to direct contact between the Vice-President and the ministers. The more confidence the Vice-President inspires in the President of the Council or the ministers, the more likely it is that the Conseil will be utilized by the government in its function of technical counselor of the government.

From the point of view of protocol, the Vice-President of the Conseil is the highest-ranking civil servant in the State. Along with the President of the Court of Cassation, he receives a higher salary than any other civil servant and at official receptions the Vice-President is qualified to speak for the whole civil service.[40]

The members of the Conseil, from the Vice-President to the Second Class Auditors, have a strong corporate spirit; all have a sense of belonging to an old and important institution. The home of the Conseil, the Palais Royal, is referred to among members as *la maison*. Among the members, regardless of their rank, there is a feeling of equality, and perfect courtesy is observed in their dealings with one another. The atmosphere of the Palais Royal is conducive to the development of a strong sense of duty which may be said to be one of the powerful unifying factors on the Conseil.

The contact of the young and the old is also advantageous—the ages of members vary from Auditors in their early twenties to Councilors of State in their sixties. All have their functions on the Conseil from the Vice-President to the Auditors who prepare the reports and defend them before the various echelons. An Auditor has the right to vote on the matter for which he is the reporter, and his vote may place the president of a section or a subsection in the minority. The constant infusion of young blood and new ideas into the Conseil keeps it in touch with the times. Young Auditors are generally encouraged to state their views, but of course there are exceptions. One such exception involved André Maginot, at that time an Auditor on the Conseil, and the imperious Alfred Picard, who was President of the Section of Public Works for six years before he became Vice-President of the Conseil in 1912. Cahen-Salvador, now a Section President, recalls the manner of Picard and the incident involving Maginot:

Many times as a young Auditor in the Section of Public Works, I have seen him [Picard] exercise his invulnerable dialectic without consideration for the unhappy reporter. At his call, Councilors, Maîtres des Requêtes, and Auditors presented their reports. He let them develop their arguments without uttering a word: then began the often painful test of the interrogation. After a few brief precise words on the litigious difficulty that the reporter had not discovered, or had treated insufficiently, he would, like a thunderbolt, state a decisive point that had not been treated. This attitude he maintained toward the oldest Councilors; he was the same with the directors of ministries who came to defend their proposals.

The meetings were sometimes painful. The timid and the bold equally excited his verve. André Maginot, a young reporter whose legendary trenchant manner surpassed that of Alfred Picard, had, in spite of the differences in rank and age, endeavored to resist the domination of his chief; President Picard had noticed some resentment on Maginot's part. On a certain day in response to a slightly impertinent defense, Picard took up with severity the attitude of his collaborator in declaring drily to him that he had not read the report but that it must be done over again within eight days in default of which he would provide for Maginot's replacement in the section.[41]

Such an attitude is exceptional on the Conseil, for when there is disagreement the element of mutual respect is seldom lacking. The above quotation also illustrates how a strong personality can influence the work of a section.

The Conseil is free from the factionalism and jockeying for position with regard to promotions that mar the serenity of many branches of the French civil service,[42] because promotion is habitually based on seniority. Promotion by seniority can lead to slothfulness and mediocrity, but these have been kept at a minimum on the Conseil; the method by which Auditors are recruited insures their capability. It is possible that unqualified personnel may enter the Conseil by appointment from outside. Abusive appointments from outside were most marked at the beginning of the century, but after 1910 several laws minimized them by requiring that the persons appointed from outside meet certain requirements of age and service in the public service.

Auditors, Maîtres des Requêtes, and Councilors have been compared to the apprentice, journeyman, and master of the gild system.[43] The comparison is an apt one. The main task of the Auditors and Maîtres des Requêtes is that of making reports. Even Councilors of State sometimes serve as reporters for important matters. The submission of the report is the first step in the Council's dealing with a matter. When any matter is submitted to the Council, whether it be legislative, administrative, or judicial, a member is assigned by the presiding officer of the section or subsection to submit a report bringing out the facts on a question. The reporter is not required to write out his report, but this is the usual practice among members of the Conseil. No contradictory facts are to be suppressed by the reporter; everything pertinent to the affair, which may have a bearing on the decision, is presented. The reporter can also present his solution; in the judicial echelons he is required to do so. In the case of legislative or administrative matters the information required by the reporter is usually obtained by personal contact with members of the ministry involved. On the assigned day the reporter gives his report to the section or subsection, either extempore or by reading the report itself, whichever is his personal preference. The discussion centers around the report and the reporter. If, during the discussion, it appears that some pertinent fact, necessary for arriving at a decision, is missing, then the reporter must unearth the missing data and present it at a later meeting. The language of the report is simple, clear, and unclouded by legal phraseology.

After discussion of the report—which may be heated—is completed, the presiding officer sums up what he believes is the prevailing opinion of the section or subsection and submits it to a vote. Of course the degree of formality in the proceedings depends partly on the character of the presiding officer. The matter is decided by a majority vote after which it is the task of the reporter to embody the decision in a subsequent report, which he submits to the presiding officer for expedition to the proper ministry. However, if the matter has to be submitted to a higher echelon of the Conseil, as bills and regulations of public administration must be, the reporter rewrites the report, substituting the decision of the section for his own solution. Before the higher echelon, usually the General Assembly, the reporter must defend the report of the section as his own, even if he is in total disagreement with it.[44]

The procedure in the judicial echelons is slightly different. In addition to the reporter there is a Government Commissioner (*Commissaire du Gouvernement*). The position of Government Commissioner attached to the judicial section was established by the ordinance of March 12, 1831, during the July Monarchy.[45] Only the month before public sessions had been instituted and petitioners before the Conseil had been granted the privilege of representation by counsel.[46] Since petitioners were to be allowed legal representation, the position of Government Commissioner was established to give the government representation on the

Conseil.[47] Although the Government Commissioner may originally have been the government's representative, his role eventually developed into one of complete independence.[48]

The Government Commissioner listens to the discussions of the subsection when the report is being discussed.[49] He has access to the dossier prepared by the reporter and to the tentative decision reached by the subsection as a result of the discussions. On the basis of these documents and what he had heard, the Government Commissioner prepares what are known as "conclusions." In his conclusions he develops both sides of the case, evaluates the facts, reviews the prior jurisprudence of the Conseil, and finally proposes a decision for or against the petitioner, stating his reasons for the proposed decision. He is not a special pleader for the State but decides according to the law and his conscience. The report and the conclusions of the Government Commissioner are read in a public session of the unit of judgment. Afterwards in a private session the case is discussed and a decision reached. The discussion centers around the proposed decisions of the subsection and of the Government Commissioner. There are many examples of decisions which are contrary to the conclusions of the Government Commissioner. Often the conclusions of the Government Commissioner, in addition to being presented in a public session, are published, especially for important or leading cases. The conclusions are only published, however, if the Government Commissioner is willing to release them. The Government Commissioner is not required to write out his conclusions; if he prefers he can submit them from notes. Because the conclusions are often published, many Government Commissioners have established their reputations in legal and governmental circles by the quality of their conclusions; among such Government Commissioners Jean Romieu, Georges Teissier, and Léon Blum have ranked high. In contrast to the judicial section where the report and conclusions are presented in public session, the advisory opinions of the administrative sections are secret. Occasionally the government will release an advisory opinion, usually to justify a course of action.

The experience and training received by members of the Conseil d'Etat, both in their functions on the Conseil and in their detached-service activities, can lead to lucrative positions in private life. Many former members of the Conseil have made their mark in public life. Among the better known are Léon Blum, who served on the Conseil for more than twenty years, André Maginot, René Mayer, and Michel Debré.

Mention should also be made of the fact that many members of the Conseil d'Etat serve on consultative commissions. These consultative commissions are attached to the various ministries in an advisory capacity. They existed throughout the Third Republic, their number steadily growing so that by 1939 there were approximately two hundred of them. For example, several of the consultative commissions attached to the Ministry of Education are: the Superior Council of Public Instruction, Consultative Committee for Primary Education, Consultative Commission for Secondary Education, Superior Council for Fine Arts, and the Superior Council for Technical Instruction.

The composition of these consultative commissions varies: some have a corporative membership, with members from various professional groups; some are composed entirely of public officials. The composition and functioning of consultative commissions are governed by their statutes, which are usually drafted by the Conseil d'Etat. Most of the members of any commission are persons who possess special knowledge or interest in the field with which the commission deals. In some cases legislation provides that a minister must consult a consultative commission before acting. Although the advice of these commissions is rarely binding on the minister, their recommendations carry great weight with him. There is a tendency for these consultative commissions to usurp the power of decision of a minister;[50] no minister, with his transient political power, likes to oppose the competence of a commission. The more important of these commissions contain one or more members from the Conseil d'Etat. A member from the Conseil d'Etat usually occupies one of the important posts on these commissions, such as presiding officer, secretary, or reporter. For example, Alfred Picard, later to become Vice-President of the Conseil d'Etat, presided over the Consultative Commission on Railroads and another Vice-President, Hébrard de Villeneuve, took part in the work on the Consultative Committee of Fine Arts, Public Assistance, and Mutuality. The most important of these commissions, the National Economic Council, a relative latecomer organized only in 1926, had, during the Third Republic, a member of the Conseil d'Etat for its Secretary-General. In 1887, members of the Conseil d'Etat belonged to more than seventy of these organizations. The collaboration of members of the Conseil d'Etat on these consultative commissions is another important way by which the influence of the Conseil permeates the administration.

The detached-service activities of members of the Conseil d'Etat have already been mentioned. Although the Conseil does not exercise any supervision or control over the duties of the members on leave, they take with them the viewpoint of the Conseil. The Conseil often provides directors of ministries or chiefs of the minister's cabinet. At the beginning of the Third Republic the maximum duration of the detached-service assignment was three years, but this period was increased several times during the Third Republic until it reached seven years. There are two methods enabling a member to be placed on detached service. One is by delegation, which cannot exceed two years, and the other is *mise hors cadres*, which could not exceed five years but was increased to ten in 1951.[51] A member delegated to a post is not replaced on the Conseil, but continues to belong to one of the sections, although he does not necessarily take part in its work. The member who is *mise hors cadres* is replaced in his functions on the Conseil, though he does not lose his seniority on which his promotions depend.

STRUCTURE OF THE CONSEIL SINCE 1940　　　　　　　　71

A good illustration of the detached-service activities which may be exercised by a member of the Conseil d'Etat is found in Pierre Tissier's book, *I Worked with Laval*.[52] Tissier, the son of the Vice-President of the Conseil d'Etat, was delegated in a minor capacity to the Ministry of Foreign Affairs shortly after he became a member of the Conseil. Later he became cabinet chief for Maurice Deligne, the Undersecretary of State for the Navy.[53] In January, 1930, he became the cabinet chief for Pierre Laval, then Minister of Labor. Tissier's predecessor as Laval's cabinet chief was René Mayer, at that time an Auditor on the Conseil. When Laval moved to the Ministry of Interior and became President of the Council of Ministers, Tissier remained his cabinet chief.[54] Tissier held all these posts before attaining the age of thirty.

Finally, the growth of the Conseil's membership should be noted. From a body of seventy-six members in 1872, the number has grown to more than one hundred and sixty. The majority of the additional personnel has been absorbed by the judicial activities of the Conseil. In 1872, the Conseil had two organs of judgment, the section and the Public Assembly. Today it has twelve.

4

THE LEGISLATIVE FUNCTION OF THE CONSEIL D'ETAT SINCE 1872

IN order to understand the part played by the Conseil d'Etat in the legislative process, it is necessary to have clearly in mind what constitutes the legislative process in France. The first step is one of initiation, which is taken by the government, that is, the President of the Council of Ministers, or by a member of the legislature. The more important category of legislation is that initiated by the government; few bills introduced by members are successful in running the legislative gauntlet.[1] The actual drafting of a government bill is usually done by a committee within a ministerial department, but subsequent action and the vote on a bill are essentially in the hands of the legislative assemblies, especially the parliamentary committees. After a bill has become law it is usually necessary to establish the technical and more detailed dispositions which provide for its application. This is accomplished by decrees and regulations of public administration issued by the government. Regulations of public administration may be considered as a kind of secondary legislation, or "delegated legislation" as it is called in Britain and the United States. Since 1872 "delegated legislation" has greatly increased and is still increasing owing to the enlarged activities of the state in modern society.

Another important post-legislative factor is the interpretation of laws. The Conseil d'Etat plays a twofold role in interpreting laws: (1) on the request of the government or the administration for advice, it ascertains the existence of a legislative provision and its meaning, or the meaning of a specific legislative text; and (2) it interprets laws in its judicial capacity. The former will be considered in this chapter; the latter will be taken up in Chapter 7 in conjunction with the judicial work of the Conseil. The role of the Conseil d'Etat with regard to decrees and regulations of public administration will be considered with the administrative work of the Conseil in the next chapter. The present chapter will deal with the Conseil's part in the legislative process.

THE LEGISLATIVE FUNCTION AND THE LAW OF 1872

Prior to 1872, the Conseil had, under several regimes, played a large role in the legislative process. During the Consulate the Conseil d'Etat was responsible for drafting all legislation; this was also true of the Conseil under the Second Republic and the Second Empire. Tradition being an important factor in French politics, there was some sentiment in the National Assembly in 1872 for employing the Conseil d'Etat to draft bills. However, consultation of the Conseil by the government or by the Assembly was left optional by the law of 1872 as finally voted. During the Third Republic the legislative function of the Conseil rested on Article 8 of the law of 1872, which provided:

The Conseil d'Etat gives its advice:
 (1) On bills of parliamentary initiative that the National Assembly judges fit to send to it;
 (2) On bills proposed by the government and submitted to the Conseil d'Etat by means of a special decree; . . . it exercises in addition, until it be otherwise ordained, all the powers which were conferred on the former Conseil d'Etat by laws and regulations which have not been abrogated. Councilors of State can be charged by the government with defending before the Assembly the bills which have been sent to the Conseil for examination.[2]

What does this text actually envisage? It depends upon the significance of the words "gives its advice," regarding which the intention of the drafters of the law of 1872 is clear. The Conseil d'Etat would, upon receiving the text of a bill from either the government or the Assembly, suggest whatever changes in the text it thought necessary to ensure correct legal form and conformity with other legislation. Thus, the role of the Conseil d'Etat would be one of legal experts giving technical assistance to the government or the Assembly. Also, the government or the Assembly could send the Conseil a request to draft the text of a bill, specifying the general provisions to be embodied in the text. The sending of a bill to the Conseil for its expert advice was entirely optional on the part of the government or the Assembly. In the event that the Assembly sent a bill to the Conseil, a vote approving the action had to be obtained in the Assembly—a complicated procedure and one which discouraged such a move. In case the government sought the advice of the Conseil, the request had to be signed by a minister. This is the practical import of the words "special decree" in Article 8, quoted above.

Article 8 also provided that the Conseil d'Etat exercise the functions, which had not been abrogated, of the former Conseil d'Etat. With regard to legislation these were of secondary importance—for example, to change the boundary of a commune or the name of a city required a legislative enactment. Prior legislation required that the advice of the Conseil d'Etat must be sought on such a bill.

Another provision stated that the government could appoint a Councilor of State to defend, before the Assembly, a bill that had been examined by the Conseil d'Etat—that is, to assume the office of a reporter. A member so designated would be expected to explain and defend any changes or additions to the text made by the Conseil d'Etat. Regarding this provision there were several adverse comments during the debates on the law, but it was accepted nevertheless.

THE LEGISLATIVE WORK OF THE CONSEIL D'ETAT DURING
THE THIRD REPUBLIC

The provisions of the law of 1872 regarding the legislative function of the Conseil d'Etat remained unchanged for the duration of the Third Republic. Now it remains to be observed how they operated in practice. Official statistics are available for the legislative work of the Conseil only for the first fifteen years of its operation (1872–87). These statistics differentiate between bills "of general interest" and bills "of local interest," the differentiation depending on whether the bill pertained to France as a whole or to a limited geographical area. A bill "of local interest" was one which, for example, enabled a particular town to borrow a million francs or more, or to modify its communal boundaries. A bill "of general interest" applied to the nation as a whole. During the period 1872–77 [3] the administrative sections of the Conseil examined 68 bills "of general interest" and 364 bills "of local interest." Of the bills "of general interest," nine were sent to the Conseil by the National Assembly; the rest of the bills "of general interest" and all of the bills "of local interest" were sent by the government.[4]

All these bills were examined by the section of the Conseil which had jurisdiction over them and were subsequently referred to the General Assembly. Following the normal procedure of the Conseil, a report was presented to the section before deliberation and a subsequent report, embodying the conclusions of the deliberation, was presented to the General Assembly.

In dealing with bills the Conseil employed several procedures which can be listed as follows: (1) unconditional adoption or adoption with minor modifications; (2) adoption with major modifications accompanied by an advisory opinion (*avis*) or report explaining the modifications proposed by the Conseil; (3) rejection accompanied by an advisory opinion or report explaining the reasons for such action.[5]

Of the 68 bills "of general interest" referred to the Conseil, 5 were rejected. Eleven of the 364 bills "of local interest" were rejected. During the same period the Conseil delivered 62 advisory opinions and 9 reports either justifying the rejection of a bill or proposing major modifications.[6]

Of course no action on a bill was binding on the legislative assemblies, but rejection of a bill by the Conseil or any modifications proposed would influence the parliamentary committee which examined the bill. For the government to try to secure the passage of a bill without regard to a rejection or to modifications proposed by the Conseil might prove difficult. A speaker would be able to invoke during the debates in the Assembly the advice of that "impartial body of experts"—the Conseil d'Etat.

For the period 1872–77 the statistics show that an appreciable, though not a large, role was played by the Conseil d'Etat in legislative matters. How do the 432 bills examined compare with the total legislative task? Figures for the period are not available, but during the Second Empire when the Conseil d'Etat examined all bills, the statistics for the five-year period 1861–65 show that the Conseil examined 2,124 bills and amendments. As a rough estimate, probably no more than 20 percent of the total number of bills was referred to the Conseil during the period 1872–77. The bills referred to the Conseil include only a small portion of the most important legislation such as the finance and army bills.

The next two five-year periods, 1878–82 and 1883–87, show a sharp decline in the number of bills "of general interest" sent to the Conseil d'Etat. The accompanying tabulation shows the decline:

Bills of General Interest	1872–77	1878–82 [7]	1883–87 [8]
Parliamentary initiative	9	2	2
Government initiative	59	44	20
	68	46	22

For the period 1883–87 the government referred, on the average, four bills "of general interest" a year to the Conseil. This can hardly be construed as giving the Conseil d'Etat a large share in the legislative process.

The number of bills "of local interest" examined by the Conseil during those two five-year periods declined slightly. The figures are:

	1872–77	1878–82	1883–87
Bills of local interest	364	363	300

Although the figures for the rest of the Third Republic are not available, it can be said that the intervention of the Conseil d'Etat in the legislative process was not very great. The legislative assemblies showed no desire to use the Conseil, preferring to rely on their own competence. From 1872 to 1887 the legislative assemblies called on the Conseil d'Etat to assist in the legislative process only thirteen times, of which only four requests were made during the last ten years of the period. These four bills were: (1) a bill relative to the conservation of historical monuments; (2) a bill concerning suspension of payments, failures, and bankruptcies; (3) a bill defining nationality; (4) a bill concerning nullification of marriages.[9] None of these can be classified as "key" legislation. Rather they are all of a legal and technical nature which, in fact, could be better dealt with by the Conseil than by the legislative assemblies. The type of bill sent to the Conseil by the government was generally more important but was usually of a complex and technical nature, such as the organization of an administrative service or the establishment of salary schedules for the various grades of public servants.

The bills "of local interest" are individually less important than the bills "of general interest"; for example, during the period 1872–77, among the bills "of local interest" 66, or one sixth of the total submitted, concerned the creation of a commune or the modification of the boundary of a commune. Many of these bills "of local interest" were in reality of an administrative character for which the legislature still retained power to act.[10] They were generally without political significance and their passage was a mere formality, after the Conseil had approved them.

The Conseil d'Etat did not always docilely accept its role as technical counselor of the government in the spirit of a nonpolitical corps ready to serve any regime. On occasion during the nineteenth century when called upon by the government on a matter of reform, the Conseil pronounced against the reform or presented a solution in absolute contradiction to the views of parliament.[11] This, however, was exceptional; when the opinion of the government or the parliament was known, the Conseil was obliged to follow.

Although no statistics are available for the period 1889–1940 on the legislative work of the Conseil d'Etat, the indications are that its participation in legislative matters was not considerable. Probably the volume of this participation declined from the small amount alluded to above for the period 1878–87. I have been assured by members of the Conseil d'Etat who served on the Conseil during the latter years of the Third Republic that the Conseil was only rarely consulted on a bill. What were the reasons for this lack of utilization of the Conseil d'Etat? The first was the unwillingness of the legislative assemblies to share their prerogative, and the second was the preference of the ministers to depend on their bureaus, which, being directly responsible to the minister, were more amenable than the Conseil d'Etat.[12]

During the Third Republic there were several bills introduced in parliament aimed at increasing the participation of the Conseil d'Etat in the legislative process.[13] All these projects invoked the lack of technical competence on the part of the legislative assemblies and the ministerial bureaus. They also pointed to the poorly drafted legislative texts which they alleged to be often obscure, contradictory, and incomplete. Some referred longingly to the omnipotent Napoleonic Conseil d'Etat of the Consulate and Empire. Authors of books on constitutional and administrative law also suggested a wider utilization of the Conseil d'Etat in legislative matters.[14]

Aside from the official consultation of the Conseil d'Etat in legislative matters, ministers, administrators, and members of parliament sometimes consulted members of the Conseil unofficially. For example, the text of the parliamentary report on the separation of church and state in 1905, which traced the relations between church and state from the baptism of Clovis to the present and which first brought Briand into the public spotlight, was alleged to have been drafted for Briand by a Maître des Requêtes, Grunebaum-Ballin.[15] Members of the Conseil occupying administrative posts while on detached service have often been in a position to draft the texts of bills.

Through detached-service activities, members of the Conseil d'Etat are to be found in various posts in the administration, but members who are not on detached service do not necessarily remain closed up in the Palais Royal. Instead, members who belong to one of the administrative sections form a floating reservoir of technicians who lend their services to the various ministries. The texts of most bills are drafted by the ministerial bureaus, and afterward they are usually submitted to a consultative commission for review. Occasionally a member of the Conseil d'Etat may be called in by a minister or bureau chief to help with the drafting of a text. Many members of the Conseil are members of the consultative commissions that review legislative texts. Thus, unofficially, members of the Conseil d'Etat are in a position to play some part in the legislative process.

The Conseil d'Etat has stayed relatively in tune with the times. During the nineteenth century, its approach to economic and social problems was within the context of economic liberalism. An example of this was the action of the Conseil as a watchdog against what was called "municipal socialism." The Conseil opposed all plans for municipal enterprise, be it public utilities, pharmacies, or free medical treatment by a community doctor. Until the attitude of the government and the parliament changed with regard to economic enterprises created by national and local authorities in competition with private citizens, the control of the Conseil over these matters was effective. The highly centralized administrative system in France made this control by the Conseil possible. This is because the limits of action of a commune, city, or department are strictly defined by statute and the control over legality is exercised by the prefects, the ministers, and the Conseil d'Etat. Before 1902,[16] any communal expenditures which required the borrowing of more than a certain sum had to be approved by law, which, prior to its enactment, had to be submitted to the Conseil d'Etat for an advisory opinion. By this means the Conseil possessed an effective veto over large expenditures for communal enterprises of a commercial or industrial nature because the advisory opinion of the Conseil on these matters was invariably followed.

The official participation of the Conseil d'Etat in the legislative process during the Third Republic was generally confined to legislation of a technical legal nature. The law on associations of 1901 is a good example, as is also the legislation "of local interest." In other words this legislation was usually of such a nature that once the approval of the Conseil had been secured, its passage by the legislative assemblies was merely a matter of form. The unofficial legislative role played by members of the Conseil on departmental drafting committees and through direct intercourse with the members of parliament cannot be determined. In conclusion, it can be said that the role of the Conseil in the legislative process during the Third Republic was small. After the defeat of 1940, official consultation of the Conseil on legislation was greatly increased.

BETWEEN THE REPUBLICS: VICHY AND FREE FRANCE

At a General Assembly of the Conseil d'Etat at Royat on August 24, 1940, Alfred Porché, the Vice-President of the Conseil d'Etat, in the presence of Raphaël Alibert, Minister of Justice and a former Maître des Requêtes, asked that the legislative function of the Conseil be increased. Porché stated that the reestablishment of the Conseil's Section on Legislation would be a precious indication that the government intended to give the Conseil d'Etat a share in the legislative process.[17] He added that the Conseil d'Etat was ready to take its place in the new regime.[18] In his address Alibert spoke of the large legislative role played by the Conseil d'Etat during the Consulate and Empire under Bonaparte and intimated that the Conseil might again be called upon to play such a role under the future, reorganized government.[19]

However, the law of December 18, 1940, on the Conseil d'Etat in dealing with the legislative function was exactly the same as the law of May 24, 1872. This law on the Conseil d'Etat was considered to be transitional; there were indications that under the projected Vichy constitution the Conseil d'Etat would be given a considerable part in the legislative process. Almost a year later, on August 19, 1941, at another General Assembly of the Conseil d'Etat at Royat, an increase in the legislative role was alluded to again by the then minister of justice, Joseph Barthélemy, in the presence of Marshal Pétain, who had come to receive the oath of allegiance to his person from the members of the Conseil.[20]

Governmental reorganization by Vichy never took place and the new constitution projected by the Vichy government was never promulgated. However, the draft constitution made no mention of the Conseil d'Etat.[21] Nevertheless, it became the practice under the Vichy government for ministers to submit all legislative projects to the examination of the Conseil d'Etat. This was a considerable change from the practice current during the Third Republic. But, for the future role of the Conseil d'Etat in the legislative process, the development of the consultative committees of the Free French government was more important.

Both the Committee on Legislation of the London period and its successor, the Juridical Committee of the Algiers period, had a large part in the drafting of texts of ordinances by which Free France was governed. From its founding in 1943 until it was replaced by the Permanent Commission in 1945, the Juridical Committee examined all proposed ordinances. The committee suggested modifications or alternate texts when it seemed advisable and acted as the censor of technical form. In the eleven months from the liberation of France until the Juridical Committee was merged with the Conseil d'Etat, it examined 892 proposed ordinances.[22] This great volume of ordinances was subjected to a more hasty examination than would have been desirable under more normal conditions. These ordinances were of primary importance and many of the texts were lengthy and complex. Some of the more important of these texts dealt with governmental organization, the nationalization of the Renault works, confiscation of illicit profits, restitution of confiscated property, prices and wages.[23] In many cases the committee substituted proposals of its own as being better suited than those presented by the government to achieve the end desired.

The ordinance of July 31, 1945, on the Conseil d'Etat transferred the attributions of the Juridical Committee to the Conseil d'Etat. This is how the Conseil d'Etat under the Fourth Republic came to have a defined part in the legislative process. Since August, 1945, the Conseil d'Etat has examined all bills of government origin. This constitutes the most important part of legislation, because, of the bills which eventually become law, those introduced by the government are superior both in quantity and importance to private member bills. Thus, since 1945 the role of the Conseil in the legislative process has increased significantly.

SINCE THE ORDINANCE OF JULY 31, 1945

After the integration of the Juridical Committee into the Conseil d'Etat as the Permanent Commission, the examination of bills of government origin was divided between that body and the administrative sections. The Permanent Commission examines all bills declared urgent and the administrative sections all others. In the first eight years of the operation of the law more than half of the bills of government origin have been declared urgent and submitted to the Permanent Commission; from 1953 until the end of the Fourth Republic, this proportion rose to two thirds. The ordinance of 1945 intended that the declaration of a bill as urgent would be an exceptional procedure, but instead the Permanent Commission examined the largest share during the Fourth Republic.[24] The declaration of urgency is made by the minister and concurred in by the President of the Council of Ministers. Then the Maître des Requêtes, who is Secretary-General of the bureau of the President of the Council, sends the text of the bill to the Permanent Commission. Bills submitted to the Permanent Commission are usually examined and returned within four days. Ordinarily, examination by an administrative section and then by the General Assembly of the Conseil requires from eight to twenty days.[25]

A factor in the large number of bills declared urgent is the desire of the government to have them examined prior to the next meeting of the Council of Ministers. If the bills that are scheduled to be taken up in the weekly meetings of the Council of Ministers were submitted to the normal procedure of examination by the administrative section and then by the General Assembly, it would delay consideration of these bills by the ministers. Obviously, given the reduced time for examination and the fact that the bill is examined by only one organ of the Conseil instead of two, the bills submitted to the Permanent Commission are less thoroughly examined than those which are submitted to the administrative sections.

Generally, the bills submitted to the examination of the Permanent Commission are of a delicate nature and are more closely related to the general policy of the government than those submitted to the administrative sections. Also, because many have been inscribed on the calendar for discussion at the next meeting of the Council of Ministers, the texts have often been hastily and inadequately prepared by the ministerial departments. Because of these factors the Permanent Commission is called upon to pronounce against the basic principles of a bill more often than are the administrative sections. Thus, the Permanent Commission is not only the "censor of form" but also the judge of basic principles. Whenever the Permanent Commission decides against the principles of a bill, it submits an alternative proposal for any features of a bill it judges inopportune or unconstitutional. By this means the Permanent Commission has also come to exercise a certain limited control over the constitutionality of bills.[26] The Permanent Commission has on numerous occasions pronounced on the compatibility of the dispositions of a bill with the Constitution.[27] It should be noted that this action is preventive; it precedes parliamentary action on a bill. Once the bill has been enacted, there is no court in France competent to pronounce on its compatibility with the Constitution.

The administrative sections and the General Assembly have also decided matters relating to the interpretation of the Constitution. These matters were submitted by the government for an advisory opinion. For example, the General Assembly was asked to clarify several points regarding the powers of the President of the Republic and the President of the Council.[28]

When an administrative section finds that the dispositions of two bills submitted by two different ministerial departments are in conflict, it usually informs the departments concerned and they are left to compromise their differences. The administrative sections will occasionally propose a solution or will arbitrate the difficulty if asked to do so. If the conflict concerns two ministerial departments for which two different sections are competent, they will meet in joint session.

The Permanent Commission is also called upon to mediate departmental conflicts, mostly on bills in an incomplete stage of development. These latter are submitted to the Permanent Commission expressly for the purpose of compromising the conflicting theses of the departments concerned.[29] Occasionally, the Permanent Commission has been called upon to examine bills already submitted to a parliamentary committee. In this case the Permanent Commission submits its advice directly to the parliamentary committee.[30]

A problem connected with the legislative process and deserving special mention because of its importance was that of decree-laws. They were issued under a parliamentary delegation of the legislative power to the executive for a limited time, and loosely confined to a specific sphere, such as finance or national defence. The law granting the power to issue decree-laws differed from an ordinary "invitation" contained in legislative acts to exercise the rule-making power in that for the decree-laws the limits within which the executive could act were not strictly defined; also, a decree-law could supersede a law, which an ordinary decree could not do. From 1926 to 1940 the power to make decree-laws was granted eleven times; in the decade 1930–40, France was governed by decree-law approximately one third of the time. In 1940, the Assemblies abdicated the legislative and constituent power to Marshal Pétain, which many professed to see as the logical culmination of the decree-law development.

Except for the decree-laws of 1926,[31] which were submitted to the Conseil for examination, the Conseil had no official part in the formulation of decree-laws. They were drafted in the ministerial departments and in the bureau of the President of the Council, though members of the Conseil d'Etat on detached service and as "floating personnel" played some part in drafting them. During the Fourth Republic the practice of issuing decree-laws returned in spite of an alleged constitutional prohibition against them. Since the Conseil d'Etat was consulted normally on these decree-laws and in some measure helped facilitate their reappearance, a brief review of the question of decree-laws is not out of place here.

There had always been some opposition on legal grounds to the "delegation" of legislative power during the Third Republic. In 1940 the delegation to Marshal Pétain of not only the legislative power but also the constituent power, placed the prewar "delegations" in an even worse light, although there was a considerable difference between the law of July 10, 1940, and the enabling acts which paved the way for the decree-laws of the 1920's and 1930's. Under the decree-laws there had always been a time limit and the possibility of parliamentary control, but not under the 1940 grant. Nevertheless, with the fall of the Vichy regime, the decree-law device was in great disfavor.

When the time came for the drafting of the Constitution of the Fourth Republic, this disfavor translated itself into Article 13 of the Constitution of 1946. Article 13 stated: "The National Assembly alone votes the law. It [the National Assembly] cannot delegate this right." The majority of the members of the Constituent Assembly understood this as a prohibition of the right of the Assembly to grant decree-law power.[32] The controversy concerning the constitutionality of decree-laws was extensive and complicated—there being almost as many different approaches as there were authors. Several jurists claimed that the wording of Article 13 did not prohibit decree-law grants.[33] To some of these persons Article 13 simply stated that the assembly could not delegate the right to vote the laws; the article was merely a tautology because "law" means a legislative enactment while a decree-law is an act of the executive.[34] For them the intention of the Constituent Assembly was neither relative nor material to the controversy; the letter of the article alone was material. However, many constitutional writers upheld the view that Article 13 did outlaw the decree-law grants.[35] Their arguments are too extensive and varied to be considered here, but a brief mention of some of their points can be made. Some of these writers appealed to the intention of the Constituent Assembly, or to the effect of the ratification of the Constitution by the naion. Others pointed out that a decree-law was a decree which modified a law, which was a contradiction of the hierarchy of laws and decrees.

Nevertheless, under the law of August 17, 1948, and again under the law of July 11, 1953, the government was given broad powers to effect economic and administrative reforms. Were the decrees isused under the law of August 17 the same as the decree-laws of the Third Republic? The government, which throughout the debates on the bill took the view that Article 13 did prohibit decree-laws, claimed that they were not. Yet these decrees modified laws. Since technically it took a law to modify a law, and the law-making power belonged solely to the parliament and could not be delegated, it has been argued that the law of August 17 was unconstitutional.[36] If one accepts this position, then the justification, which will be considered in a moment, advanced by the government to parliament that the law did not provide for the prohibited decree-laws was merely a subterfuge. However, even if the Constitution had been violated by the law of August

17, there was no authority which could invalidate a parliamentary enactment.

The bill which became the law of August 17 was examined by the Permanent Commission of the Conseil d'Etat which "deemed that the bill did not involve a genuine delegation of legislative power, but it [the Permanent Commission] proposed modifications which had for their purpose the avoidance of all confusion with the laws granting *pleins pouvoirs* before 1940." [37] To try and allay the suspicion of the Assembly, the Conseil d'Etat inserted in the text of the bill the words that certain matters "transferred" from the legislative to the executive power naturally belonged to the autonomous rule-making power (*réglementaire par nature*). The Conseil also changed the wording of Article 6 so that the decrees issued by the executive would take precedence over "provisions now in force" (*dispositions en vigueur*) instead of over "law" (*loi*) as contained in the original bill.[38]

The justification formulated by the Conseil d'Etat—and later advanced by the government in parliament—to show that the bill did not provide for decree-laws was based on the view that the bill merely provided for a redrawing of the boundary between the autonomous rule-making power (*pouvoir réglementaire*) of the executive and the area covered by legislative enactments. This view would have been more plausible if all the powers "delegated" by the law of August 17 were permanent; but such was not the case. In reality, the law can be divided into two parts: one providing for a permanent "delegation," or "redrawing" of the boundary between the legislative and rule-making power, and another providing for a "delegation" for a limited time of certain powers to effect financial reforms. The government did not face the issue during the debates that there were two different aspects of the grant—the permanent and the temporary. There was little difference between the temporary grant provided in this law and the enabling acts of the Third Republic.

The opinion of the Permanent Commission of the Conseil

d'Etat that the bill did not provide for a delegation of the legislative power was invoked during the debates in Parliament by both the President of the Council, André Marie, and the Minister of Finance, Paul Reynaud.[39] The justification advanced by the Permanent Commission in its desire to aid the government may be considered as a form of legal casuistry. The government was forced by a combination of economic necessity and the impotence of Parliament to seek special powers. Political necessity forbade that the grant be called "decree-law power," a type of grant presumably prohibited by the Constitution. Therefore, the Permanent Commission suggested the solution described above, which would make it seem that the government was not requesting powers similar to the unpopular decree-law grants of the latter years of the Third Republic. Exemplifying the political nature of the controversy was the position of René Capitant, a jurist, on Article 13 at the time it was formulated and his position during the debates on the law of August 17. During the elaboration of the text of the draft Constitution in the Committee set up for that purpose by the first Constituent Assembly, Capitant, a member of the Committee, argued that Article 13 did not prohibit the decree-law grants.[40] However, in August of 1948, being a leading deputy of de Gaulle's *Rassemblement du Peuple Français*, he argued that such grants were prohibited.[41]

In the early part of 1953 the government pledged itself to work for a revision of the Constitution. As an initial step, the Conseil d'Etat was consulted on the meaning of several articles of the Constitution, among them Article 13. The advisory opinion of the Conseil d'Etat delivered on February 6, 1953, the complete text of which is to be found in Appendix A, stated that Article 13 did prohibit decree-laws. But the Conseil recognized the right of the legislature to transfer competence for most matters to the executive, thus maintaining the position it took with regard to the law of August 17. But, as has already been pointed out, the law of August 17 did provide for a delegation of legislative power in the Third Republic manner.[42] Since 1948, as will be seen, there have been other examples of such delegations. The Conseil also recognized that decrees having legislative force could be issued under a law which stated the general principles and limits to which the decrees would adhere. This type of "delegation" or basic law is called a *loi-cadre,* and its legality is recognized by such critics as René Capitant.

Whereas the decree-laws of the Third Republic escaped, with one exception, the scrutiny of the Conseil d'Etat, the decrees issued under the law of August 17 were submitted to the Conseil d'Etat. Article 6 of the law of August 17 expressly provided that all decrees issued under the law must be submitted for advice to the Conseil d'Etat. This provision was to insure that decrees were within the limits of the enabling act and that the drafting was in good form.

In 1953, by the law of July 11, the Laniel government was granted special powers. This grant had three aspects: (1) it extended the scope of the permanent "delegation" of the law of August 17 as the government had requested, but the Assembly imposed a time limit; [43] (2) it gave the executive the power to limit, suspend, or defer expenditures; (3) it gave the executive the right to reform certain financial legislation and certain branches of the public service, including the Conseil d'Etat itself. The law provided that the government had to solicit the advice of the Conseil on decrees pertaining to matters in the first and third categories. These powers were conferred on the existing government only and were limited to a specific period of time.

The debates on the law of July 11, 1953, pertained almost entirely to the political aspects of the delegation; little was said about the constitutional aspects, in contrast to the debates on the law of August 17, 1948. The same was true of the decree-law grants during the Third Republic; only those of 1924 and 1926 gave rise to debate on the constitutional aspects. After 1953, special powers were granted with increasing frequency. Generally grants of "special powers" (*pouvoirs spéciaux*), which was the term used to designate these grants in the Fourth Republic, were limited to the government in function and for a specific period of time. The Conseil d'Etat had to be consulted on most of the decrees provided for by the enabling acts. Thus, the Fourth Republic was unsuccessful in trying to avoid the use of this device.

The Constitution of the Fifth Republic sanctions the legality of "special powers." Article 38 of the Constitution permits parliament to authorize special powers for a limited period of time, which ends all question of the legality of such grants. The enabling act allows the government to issue "ordinances" covering matters that are normally within the domain of law. Article 38 also requires that these ordinances be examined by the Conseil d'Etat.

The accompanying tabulation gives the number of bills or ordinances, and also the number of decrees promulgated under the law of August 17 and subsequent grants, examined by the Conseil since Liberation: [44]

	Bills			Decrees, Issued under the Law of August 17 and Subsequent Grants, Administrative Section
	Permanent Commission	Administrative Section	Total	
1944–45 [45]	892	—	892	
1945–46 [46]	500	266	766	
1946–47	220	183	403	
1947–48	246	141	387	
1948–49	215	136	347	100
1949–50	104	179	283	67
1950–51	121	118	239	60 [47]
1951–52	149	118	267	34
1952–53	105	97	202	36
1953–54	131	69	200	192 [48]
1954–55	145	64	209	460 [49]
1955–56	122	48	170	149 [50]
1956–57	109	93	201	244
1957–58	53	51	104 [51]	196 [52]

The decrease in the number of bills examined by the Conseil d'Etat is mainly owing to two factors: the settling of problems arising out of the war and the increasing tendency to grant special powers to the government.

The role of the Conseil d'Etat in the legislative process is a valuable aid to the government, both in insuring the correct legal form of bills and bringing to the attention of the government any inconveniences or illegalities that the text may contain. This is a role which the Conseil d'Etat is well fitted to perform because of its competence in the technicalities of legislation. As a result of the work of the Conseil d'Etat, the legislative texts of the Fourth Republic were better drafted than those of the Third. There will probably be further improvement in the Fifth Republic owing to restrictions on the power of the legislature to amend government bills. The legislative function of the Conseil d'Etat is only one aspect of the role of the Conseil as technical counselor of the government. The other aspect, the administrative function, is the subject of the next chapter.

5

THE ADMINISTRATIVE FUNCTION OF THE CONSEIL D'ETAT SINCE 1872

THE administrative function of the Conseil d'Etat as technical counselor of the government, as is the case with its legislative function, except for bills declared urgent, is performed entirely by the administrative sections and the General Assembly. The work of the administrative sections of the Conseil is entirely separate from the Judicial Section and the work of the one does not in any way prejudice the work of the other. Even though an administrative section, in its capacity of technical counselor of the government, has examined and approved a decree, the same decree can be declared *ultra vires* and annulled by one of the judicial echelons of the Conseil.

The administrative function of the Conseil is a consultative one. Though in many cases the advice of the Conseil d'Etat must be solicited, only rarely is the administration required to follow the Conseil's advice. The administration will often, of its own volition, ask the Conseil for advice. Consultation of the Conseil is desirable because, as has been said above, the members of the Conseil are highly trained legal technicians with practical experience in the administrative field. As also noted before, the administrative sections of the Conseil are themselves specialized, each section being competent to expedite the matters sent by certain ministerial departments. The administrative matters referred to the Conseil can be divided into two general classes: (1) those on which the Conseil d'Etat must obligatorily be consulted, and (2) those on which the Conseil d'Etat may optionally be consulted.

OBLIGATORY CONSULTATION OF THE CONSEIL D'ETAT

The Conseil d'Etat must be consulted on all regulations of public administration (*règlements d'administration publique*).[1] The power to make regulations of public administration is part of the rule-making power of the executive, a power which, during the Third Republic, belonged theoretically to the President of the Republic. This power was transferred under the Constitution of 1946 to the President of the Council of Ministers. The Constitution of 1958, with certain exceptions, vests this power in the Premier. Regulations of public administration are issued on the "invitation" of the parliament and their content concerns the details of execution of a law. For a law organizing a public service of any kind, the regulation of public administration would determine, usually, the agency of enforcement, the composition of the agency of enforcement, and the duties and the limits of the powers of each. The text of the law "invites" the executive to make a regulation of public administration by the following formula, which is usually inserted at the end of a law: "A regulation of public administration will determine the measures of execution of the present law." This formula is not considered as a delegation of the rule-making power but rather as an invitation to the executive to exercise his autonomous rule-making power. A regulation of public administration can be modified only by another regulation of the same type, or by a law, because a law is above a regulation of public administration in the hierarchy of laws and decrees. One procedural requirement is that the regulation must be submitted to the Conseil d'Etat for examination. If this procedural requirement is not followed, if the Conseil d'Etat is not consulted, then the regulation may be annulled by the Conseil d'Etat in its judicial capacity for failure to observe procedures required by law.

The existence of regulations of public administration dates from the year VIII (1800); they are also specifically mentioned in the Constitution of the Second Republic. Article 8 of the law of May 24, 1872, includes the examination of all regulations of public administration among the functions of the Conseil d'Etat. This provision is also repeated in the law of December 18, 1940, and the ordinance of July 31, 1945, on the Conseil. Before 1900, legal theorists considered that regulations of public administration constituted a delegation of legislative power. But after 1900, led by the constitutional lawyer Adhémar Esmein, French opinion rejected this theory and claimed that regulations of public administration were based on the direct ordaining power of the executive; the legislative clause in a law providing that a regulation of public administration would complete the law was only an "invitation" to the executive to exercise his direct ordaining power.[2] This important shift in doctrine paved the way for the Judicial Section of the Conseil to annul a regulation of public administration in 1907.[3]

Regulations of public administration are drafted, as are government bills, in the bureaus of the ministries. Members of the Conseil d'Etat may be found on the drafting committees, but their membership there is unrelated to their official work on the Conseil. From the ministerial department the regulations are sent to the bureau of the Vice-President of the Conseil d'Etat and from there referred to the competent section. After examination by a section, all regulations of public administration must also be examined by the General Assembly of the Conseil. Proposed modifications must be approved by a majority vote. The regulation is examined to see: (1) if it reflects the intent of parliament, (2) whether or not it is within the limits of the law it is supposed to execute, (3) if the measures provided for in the regulation are adequate for the task they are expected to perform, (4) if the regulation is in harmony with other legislation and regulations, and (5) if the technical phraseology is correct.

After examination by the General Assembly, the regulation is returned to the government for promulgation. Then the regulation can either be promulgated in the form suggested by the Conseil d'Etat or, if the government does not wish to promulgate the regulation in that form, it must be promulgated in the original form in which it was sent to the Conseil. If the government does not follow either of these courses, the regulation is liable to annulment by the judicial section of the Conseil for *ultra vires* on the ground of failure to observe procedures required by law.

The only regulations of public administration whose texts are drafted by the Conseil are those concerning the Conseil itself or pertaining to the administrative jurisdiction. Although not based on any statutory provision, it is traditional that the Conseil draft the regulations which pertain to its own organization and functioning.

In addition to regulations of public administration, the executive must also consult the Conseil before issuing decrees in the form of regulations of public administration (*décrets en forme de règlement d'administration publique*). The name "decree in the form of a regulation of public administration" is given to decrees regulating certain matters, enumerated by law, which the law requires the government to submit to the Conseil d'Etat for advice. They are issued on the "invitation" of parliament, but, unlike the regulation of public administration, their purpose is not to complete immediately a particular law but to deal with specific events of an individual nature which may arise from time to time. For example, the law of associations of July 1, 1901, provided that all declarations of public utility of an association must be made by a decree in the form of a regulation of public administration (Article 10).

In addition to regulations of public administration and decrees in the form of regulations of public administration, which must undergo the double examination of the section and the General Assembly, there is a whole host of matters which diverse laws require to be submitted to the Conseil, where examination by one of the administrative sections is sufficient. A decree issued under such conditions is called a "decree in the Conseil d'Etat" (*décret en Conseil d'Etat*). It is not general in scope. For example, the authorization for public institutions to accept gifts or to be the beneficiaries of wills is granted by a decree in the Conseil d'Etat. For this the examination of a single section, the Section of Interior in this case, is sufficient, although at the request of a section the matter could be submitted to the General Assembly. Another example is a mining concession. In France, the exploitation of all subsoil wealth by private individuals or concerns must be authorized by the State. This authorization must be given by a decree in the Conseil d'Etat. Decrees in the Conseil d'Etat are usually of an individual, not a general, nature.

Ordinarily, the government is not required to follow the advice of the Conseil d'Etat, but in some instances the law provides that a decree must be issued *in conformance with* the advice of the Conseil d'Etat. For example, the finance law of July 13, 1911, provided that the mutation or transfer of a mining concession could not be effected except in conformance with the advice of the Conseil d'Etat (Article 138). In general, matters such as these are examined only by a single administrative section.

OPTIONAL CONSULTATION OF THE CONSEIL D'ETAT

In addition to the matters on which the Conseil must be consulted, there are matters on which the Conseil is consulted on the option of the ministerial department. The matters on which the ministries consult the Conseil of their own volition fall into two general categories: (1) decrees, and (2) advice. In the hierarchy of legal texts the decree follows law, ordinance, decree-law, regulation of public administration, decree in the form of a regulation of public administration, and decree in the Conseil d'Etat. Decrees are numerous; they are employed for such things as individual appointments to an administrative post, the rules that the lower echelons of the administration are to follow in the application of laws and regulations of public administration, and the minute internal operation of a ministry.

The Conseil examines these decrees for their phraseology, continuity, and advisability, as they do regulations of public administration. It is an advantage to the ministry to submit them to the Conseil, because if an administrative section has examined them for legality, it is less likely that the Judicial Section will find cause to annul them for *ultra vires*. The submission of these decrees to the Conseil also relieves the bureau officials of a certain amount of work, which in many cases would involve painstaking research. It is conceivable that the consultation of the Conseil adds to the slowness of a proverbially slow administration, but because the consultation is optional, the officials of a ministry only consult the Conseil d'Etat when they are in doubt and wish to take precautions. This practice developed only toward the end of the nineteenth century, for in the early years of the Third Republic the Conseil was often consulted on decrees as a matter of course. The result was that the Conseil had much of its time consumed by matters of secondary importance. In the twentieth century the growth of the public services made it impossible to consult the Conseil on every detail. Since then, the decrees on which the Conseil has been consulted have been fewer in number and greater in importance.

The administrative departments often request the legal advice of the Conseil d'Etat. They might inquire if the provisions of a certain law or regulation are still in force or if they have been modified or annulled by a subsequent law or regulation. The Conseil might be asked to determine what are the laws, regulations, and decrees currently in force on a certain specified point, or if a certain reform can be accomplished by a decree or a regulation of public administration, instead of by a law. In a case such as the latter the Conseil would search for a solution which would not force the department to apply to the parliament for a legislative solution, because the parliament is slow and the measures would also run the risk of being altered by the legislator.

For example, in 1899 when the problem of automobile traffic was first making itself felt, the government wished to regulate it by means of decrees instead of applying to the parliament for legislation.

The government, which did not wish to ask the parliament to legislate on the matter, asked several Councilors of State for an official advisory opinion. They [the Councilors of State] endeavored to attach the regulatory power, in the absence of any formal text, to the head of the State by Articles 94 and 99 of the law of April 5, 1884.[4]

Articles 94 and 99 were interpreted by the Conseil as giving the mayor of the commune and the prefect of the department the right to issue regulations to control automobile traffic, although the regulation of automobile traffic was not specifically mentioned or even foreseen in 1884. From this the Conseil reasoned that if in this matter the mayor had the right to issue regulations for the commune, and the prefect for the department, then the President of the Republic logically had this power, a fortiori, for the national territory. Obviously this conclusion involved "legal acrobatics."[5] Nevertheless, the government took advantage of it to issue decrees regulating not only the operation but also the construction of automobiles.

This attribution of power to the executive was challenged as illegal before the judicial section of the Conseil; in 1919, the Conseil in its judicial capacity, sustained the solution of the administrative sections by ruling that: "[this power] belongs to the head of the State, outside of any legislative delegation and by virtue of his own powers. . . ."[6] Thus, without any legislation on the subject, the Conseil encouraged the government to assume this power as part of the autonomous rule-making power of the President of the Republic and twenty years later approved this assumption of power by a judicial decision.

The advice given by the Conseil as the result of consultation is, in principle, confidential. Only if the minister sees fit to make the advice public does it become known. The minister may do this in order to justify the course of action the ministry has taken or to clarify certain situations to administrators or to the public. Many of the advisory opinions find their way into administrative circulars which serve as guides to the administrator; thus an advisory opinion can become part of departmental policy. Occasionally the advice given by the Conseil is published in the *Journal Officiel* or in the semi-official *Revue générale d'administration*.[7] Thus it is possible to examine a specimen of this advice for its form.

In 1894, the Ministry of Education consulted the Conseil for advice on five questions relating to the salary and classification of teachers. For example, the fifth question read: "Is the second disposition of Article 71 of the law of January 26, 1892, abrogated by the law of July 20, 1893?" The Conseil d'Etat in an advisory opinion of December 27, 1894 came to the following conclusion:

> The second classification of Article 71 of the law of January 26, 1892, by virtue of which the indemnity of residents must be added integrally to the legal salary in cities of more than 100,000 inhabitants, and not to the guaranteed salary, is irreconcilable with the rules set forth by the new Article 32, which places integrally at the charge of the State the payment of the said guaranteed salary.
> Hence, the disposition of the law of January 26, 1892, was abrogated by the law of July 20, 1893, when the latter modified Article 32 of the law of July 19, 1889.[8]

In the foregoing advisory opinion the Conseil was interpreting a law, determining just what provisions were in force on a certain point, and deciding where the parliament had been silent. The advice of the Conseil is always supported by reasons which are presented briefly and succinctly.

The secrecy of the advice given by the Conseil d'Etat has recently been criticized. At present decrees and regulations when promulgated are headed by the formula "The Conseil d'Etat having been heard" (*le Conseil d'Etat entendu*), which signifies only that the Conseil has examined the text. It has been suggested that this traditional formula ought to be replaced, and that the advice of the Conseil should be made public:

Making public the advice of the Conseil d'Etat, together with an explanation of the Conseil's reasons, would constitute an effective guarantee both for the proper management of the public service and for the citizens. French public law still has important progress to make on this point. It would be necessary to replace in the drafting of decrees the present formula: "Heard in the Conseil d'Etat" (indicating that the advice of the Conseil d'Etat has been requested) with the formula: "Conforming (or contrary) to the advice of the Conseil d'Etat"; and to obligate the government when it does not follow the advice of the Conseil d'Etat to state and explain the reasons for its divergence.[9]

THE CONSULTATIVE WORK OF THE CONSEIL D'ETAT

So far only the types of administrative matters sent to the Conseil d'Etat have been discussed. The question of how significant the intervention of the Conseil is in these matters is difficult to determine because the work of the Conseil d'Etat is seldom made public.

In France, which since Napoleonic times has been highly centralized, where local governmental units are given little opportunity for independent action, where the economic life has been tightly controlled by all kinds of restrictive regulations, where religious and cultural groups have needed government authorization to operate—in short, in a country where the administration exercises such an extensive or potential control over the everyday life of the citizen, it is important that the country be well and smoothly administered. The administration should never be allowed to slacken or fall into slovenly habits; the laws and regulations should be applied with a maximum of common sense. That this has been to some extent true in France is, in part, owing to the Conseil d'Etat.

Since its founding in 1800 the Conseil has played a large part in many branches of French life, such as local government. Another sphere over which the Conseil has exercised a rather continuous influence is religion. The cultural and economic life of the country is affected by the work of the Conseil; first the Conseil tried to insure free enterprise, but since 1945 it has facilitated the operation of a mixed economy. The Conseil has also protected the rights of civil servants and at the same time confined their activities within strict legal limits.

The Conseil's role in the municipal life of France is a varied one. The prefect has the power to annul decisions of a municipal council when he considers the decision beyond the legal powers of the council. The Section of Interior of the Conseil is sometimes consulted by the ministry on whether or not the decision should be annulled by the prefect. There are also cases where the decision of the municipal council, to become effective, needs the approval of the Minister of Interior; the Conseil, Section of Interior, is often consulted on these matters. The advice of the Conseil is solicited on points of administrative policy as well as points of legality. On legal questions the advice of the Conseil is always accepted by the ministry and it is rarely disregarded on questions of policy, or on questions concerning the expediency of a measure.

During the Third Republic, the Conseil examined and gave its advice on proposals for a commune to contract long-term loans or to levy extraordinary taxation. In these matters the Conseil had to investigate the situation and to decide if the loan or taxation were necessary. Proposals to modify the territorial limits of a commune or to change its name also had to be examined by the Conseil d'Etat. The Conseil has consistently opposed all tendencies toward the multiplication of communes.

The Conseil d'Etat provides model contracts for use by the municipal authorities. These contracts will serve for almost any contingency that arises. If the municipal authority does not use the model provided by the Conseil d'Etat, the authority which must approve the contract is higher. For example, if in a certain matter the local authority uses the model provided by the Conseil d'Etat, then the contract may be approved by a prefect; however, if the local authority does not employ the model contract, a decree in the Conseil d'Etat may be necessary to approve the contract. The Conseil also has a hand in town planning, the acceptance of bequests by a commune, and in seeing that the local authorities comply in maintaining land and buildings used by the central government, but whose maintenance is the duty of the local authorities.

Before 1905, the Conseil d'Etat registered papal bulls and other acts of the Vatican. The Conseil was also charged with the authorization of religious congregations and the verification of their statutes. Double examination by the section and the General Assembly was required for the authorization of religious congregations. Both of these functions were taken from the Conseil—the registration of papal bulls by the law of separation of church and state in 1905, and the authorization of religious congregations by the law of associations of 1901. However, in 1918, with the return of Alsace-Lorraine, the Conseil resumed the registration of papal bulls for those provinces.

The original bill on associations, which was drafted in the Conseil d'Etat by a special commission formed especially for that purpose and under the chairmanship of the then Vice-President of the Conseil, Georges Coulon,[10] provided that authorization for all associations, religious and others, be given by the Conseil d'Etat. However, in the law as it was finally voted, this was reduced only to new establishments of authorized religious congregations. The founding of any new establishments by an authorized congregation was effected by a decree in the Conseil d'Etat. The initial authorization of a congregation under the law of associations required an affirmative vote by the parliament.[11] The details of execution of the law were left to a regulation of public administration which the Conseil made as advantageous as possible to the church.[12] However, political pressures counteracted the conciliatory work of the Conseil and the parliamentary majority turned the law of associations into a "law of combat" against the church.[13] The law was employed to eliminate a large number of schools operated by the clergy. The worsening relations between the French government and the Vatican led to the law of separation of church and state in 1905.

The law of separation of church and state provided for the formation of "religious associations" (*associations cultuelles*) organized among the faithful to take over the management of church property. In the eventuality that the prefect refused to recognize the "religious association," the final decision was to be made by decree in the Conseil d'Etat. The withdrawal of recognition of a "religious association" was to be decided in the same way. However, the Catholics refused to form "religious associations" and the Pope in his encyclical *Vehementer* attacked the "religious associations" as contrary to the hierarchical principles of the Roman Church. To get around the difficulty a law passed in 1907 gave clear title to most of the church property to the communes, with the proviso that the faithful were to have the right to use it.[14]

The law of 1905 was considered by most of its supporters as a militant anti-clerical measure. However, the Conseil, in the interpretation and execution of the law, attempted to soften its application. In its judicial capacity, the Conseil repeatedly affirmed the liberty of religious services and protected this right from the encroachments of overzealous mayors.

With the return of Alsace-Lorraine to France at the end of the First World War, the religious problem arose anew. The Germans had preserved the system of church and state relations which they found in Alsace-Lorraine in 1870 and trouble came when the French government attempted to apply French laws in the returned provinces. This time an advisory opinion of the Conseil d'Etat, in December 1923, helped appease the fears of the Papacy and the "religious associations" were allowed to be formed in Alsace-Lorraine under the terms of the law of 1905.[15] This advisory opinion of the Conseil improved immeasurably the relations with the Vatican and avoided, at least temporarily, a religious struggle in the returned provinces.

The functions of the Conseil relating to the economic life of France are numerous and varied. Aside from the constant consultation of the administrative sections on varied problems of finance, public works, and, more recently, problems concerning nationalization of industry and economic planning, there is a host of matters on which the Conseil must be consulted and over which the power of the Conseil is considerable. Mention will be made of some of the more important ones.

As has already been said, a concession for the exploitation of a mine is granted by a decree in the Conseil d'Etat, a function which the Conseil has performed since 1810. Until the twentieth century all mining concessions were in the hands of private enterprise. The concession grant, which allows the individual or company to exploit the mine, contains regulations concerning the nature of the operation, provides for a payment to the proprietor of the topsoil, and arranges for the State to share in the profits of the mine. The cancellation of a concession, should the concessionaire fail to adhere to the terms of the grant, is also accomplished by a decree in the Conseil d'Etat. Exploitation of mines by the State, made possible by the law of September 9, 1919, was also contingent on a decree in the Conseil d'Etat. The renewal of concessions, which after 1919 ceased to be perpetual, was accomplished in the same manner. In the case of coal mines, the nationalization of most of the coal industry in 1945 automatically removed all except small mines from the regime of concessions.

In the granting of concessions the Conseil d'Etat had to formulate general criteria which the concessionaire had to meet, to decide in what event the request for a concession should be refused, to take into account the ability of the concessionaire to exploit the concession, and also to investigate market possibilities.[16] All this requires that the Conseil conduct a thorough investigation of every request before granting the concession. The very nature of the factors to be considered, such as market possibilities, gave the Conseil large discretionary power over whether or not the concession should be granted.

With some differences, the Conseil d'Etat played a similar role for concessions to produce electricity. In transportation, permission to build streetcar lines and interurban railways, until 1880, were granted by decree in the Conseil d'Etat. After 1880 the concession for an interurban railway had to be granted by a law, but it was provided that the advice of the Conseil must be solicited on the bill. After 1886, the granting of a concession for a streetcar line was provided by a decree in the form of a regulation of public administration, which necessitates the deliberation of the General Assembly as well as the section. The Conseil also played a large part in the elaboration and execution of the Freycinet Plan, a large public works program of the eighties. During the latter part of the nineteenth century, problems connected with railroads came to form a large part of the work of the Section of Public Works. In more recent times the Conseil has dealt with problems of abandonment of service on uneconomic lines of public transport; it has had to determine if abandonments were possible or if service should be maintained in the general interest.[17]

The Conseil also has made investigations preliminary to the granting of concessions to supply natural gas to cities. The recommendations of the Conseil in these matters were only rarely unconfirmed by ministerial action. The Conseil performed a similar role when electricity began to displace gas as a means of lighting. The competition of electricity with gas gave rise to complicated problems which at first the Conseil solved by granting the concession to the cheapest supplier, until the superiority of electricity was firmly established.

During the period preceding the First World War the Conseil was adamant in its desire to keep such concessions in the hands of private enterprise. By a series of advisory opinions between 1880 and 1900, most of them coming from the Section of the

Interior, the Conseil pronounced firmly against the establishment of any publicly owned or operated commercial or industrial enterprise by a commune or a department.

There is the example of Roubaix, where the municipal council, the majority of whose members between 1892 and 1900 were adherents of municipal socialism, decided to establish a municipal pharmacy. The Conseil d'Etat, Section of the Interior, consulted by the Ministry of the Interior, by an advisory opinion of July 17, 1894, declared that the establishment of such a municipal pharmacy was beyond the powers of the municipal council.[18] The Section of the Interior based its opinion on the law of April 5, 1884, on the communes. It should be noted that nothing specific in the law of 1884 forbade this type of municipal enterprise, but in deciding as it did, the Conseil was only concurring with the prevailing philosophy on economic policy. The culmination of these advisory opinions on municipal enterprise came in March, 1900, with an advisory opinion (on a bill) on a proposal of the city of Lille to establish its own sewage disposal plant. The Conseil, in its advisory opinion, rejected the proposal because "an enterprise of this nature constitutes a commercial and industrial operation which does not fall, in principle, within the powers of the municipal councils." The advisory opinion went on to add:

That if, in fact, some cities had been authorized to assure the drinking water supply in certain cases by means of a public corporation [*régie directe*,] or very exceptionally, public and private lighting, it is by reasons of economic circumstances which permit only the city itself practically to pursue and realize the totality of necessary operations.[19]

The effect of this advice concerning the operation of a commercial or industrial enterprise by a local government, though less rigid and with numerous exceptions, remains valid until the present day. In its judicial capacity the Conseil has backed up this prohibition by its jurisprudence.[20]

The Conseil d'Etat also examined authorizations for the formation of life insurance companies as well as modifications in the statutes of companies established prior to 1807, until the law of March 17, 1905, suppressed the requirement for these authorizations. Concessions for the draining of marshes and the building of dams are also submitted to the Conseil for examination and advice. The approval of tolls on bridges and the action to rebuy such a concession is accomplished by a decree in the Conseil d'Etat. Authorizations for the founding of Chambers of Commerce, as well as the establishment of certain other associations, must be submitted to the Conseil for advice.

An association in France is an organization which operates on a nonprofit basis, as for example the Red Cross, the Bar Association, and the National Committee against Alcoholism. The law of associations of 1901 recognized three types of associations: (1) simple association, a type not declared or officially known to the government; (2) declared association, a type registered at the Ministry of Interior, existing as a legal person and having the right to acquire property to fulfill its purpose; (3) establishments of public utility, a type which must submit its statute to the Conseil d'Etat for approval, and which has the right to receive gifts and legacies—its main advantage over a declared association. The Ministry of Interior, which formally recognizes an association as an establishment of public utility, always accepts the advice of the Conseil d'Etat. The Conseil has developed criteria for recognition and compels the association to accept a standard statute. Every year the Section of the Interior of the Conseil, which handles these matters, receives approximately one hundred requests for recognition.[21]

After the Second World War, the Conseil was called upon to examine most of the statutes of the nationalized industries. These statutes were examined article by article both in the sections and in the General Assembly. The Conseil was also consulted on the new statutes of banks, the Bourse, and the *Crédit foncier*. Generally, proposals relating to economic matters arrive from a ministry which has studied them only in relation to itself. It is the duty of the Conseil to investigate the repercussions such proposals would have on other segments of the economy and to bring them to the attention of the ministry. Thus the Conseil plays a role of coordination among the ministries. If the Conseil does not have the power, legally, to oppose a proposal, it often addresses a note to the government pointing out the inconveniences and suggesting other solutions.[22]

The law of August 17, 1948, dealing with financial recovery required that all decrees issued under it be submitted to the Conseil d'Etat for advice. Concerning the economic role in general, a member of the Conseil has written:

To convince oneself of the importance of the role of the Conseil d'Etat in economic matters, it is enough to consult any of the calendars of the General Assembly on Thursday. Almost always one will find inscribed matters concerning nationalizations, basic products such as petroleum, transportation, organs of mixed economy, and agriculture. These matters do not pertain only to the public service; private industry is also affected, sometimes a specific company; when one treats the organization of commerce or agriculture, the future of innumerable small enterprises is involved.[23]

In summary, it can be said that although the Conseil has little final power of decision over economic matters, its advice is seldom ignored.

The Conseil d'Etat acted as a guardian for the assemblies in the overseas territories of the French Union created after 1946. The National Assembly, after liberation, took a greater interest in the overseas territories. No longer were practically all colonial matters to be dealt with by executive decree. Overseas assemblies were set up in an effort to associate the native populations in the process of government. However, the power given to the overseas assemblies, as is the case with the municipal and departmental councils of metropolitan France, was limited. The Conseil exercised an effective control over these embryonic creations, ensuring that they operated within the limits of their powers. On certain matters the intervention of the Conseil in the affairs of these assemblies was regular and automatic. For example, decisions governing the incidence and collection of taxes were not executory until approved by a decree in the Conseil d'Etat. The Conseil's Section of Finance had to act on these matters within ninety days after the overseas assembly's deliberation arrived at the Ministry of Overseas France.[24] Tariffs voted by the overseas assemblies became executory if they had not been annulled by the Conseil within ninety days.[25] The Conseil had the power to make substitutions in the budget; it could add expenditures or taxation.

The Conseil also exercised a control over the legality of the acts of the assemblies. The acts of overseas assemblies were annulled by a decree in the form of a regulation of public administration.[26] The Conseil was both benevolent and firm in its policy toward the overseas assemblies. The Conseil recognized that these assemblies were inexperienced; therefore the Conseil did not annul for illegality an act that failed to observe procedures required by law. On the other hand, the Conseil firmly prevented the assemblies from interfering in overseas administration. The Conseil's close contact with these assemblies enabled it to suggest to the government many reforms that could be made in legislating for and administering overseas territories.[27]

The Conseil was consulted often by the government on overseas matters. The Conseil was consulted by the government on the question if members of the assembly of the French Union, which met at Versailles, should be paid; the Conseil decided that under the terms of Articles 23 and 70 of the Constitution, they should receive a salary equivalent to that of the members of the Council of the Republic.[28] The Conseil also decided that the citizens of the overseas territories should have the same right of access to the civil service as Frenchmen.[29]

The Constitution of 1958 further liberalized the relationship of France with her overseas units. Most of the former overseas territories became autonomous republics associated with France in the newly created French Community. The autonomous republics were better prepared to assume their new position, having experienced a measure of self-government under the Fourth Republic. In addition to the twelve autonomous republics, all in Africa, there remain the overseas departments, a number of overseas territories, and Algeria, whose status is uncertain. The overseas departments and territories are tied closely to metropolitan France, and here the Conseil's role remains as it was under the Fourth Republic.

The Conseil plays a large role in matters concerning the civil service. The Conseil is always consulted on changes in the statutes governing civil servants. Most of the statutes of the hundreds of consultative councils, which are attached to the various ministries, were submitted to the Conseil for examination. Traditionally, the Conseil has been called upon to codify diverse laws and decrees. It was under the First Empire that the Section of Interior drafted the famous *Code Civil*. Recently the Conseil examined the nine codes which constitute the General Code of Taxation, established in 1950.[30]

The role of the Conseil d'Etat in coordinating the legislative policies of the ministerial departments has been alluded to in the previous chapter. The role of coordination performed by the Conseil in administrative matters is much the same. Given the prestige of the Conseil in the ministries, its advice is almost always followed.

The administrative sections help insure the legality of administrative action through the examination of regulations and decrees, and by advice. The effort of the administrative sections to insure legality of action is generally anterior to the action itself. After administrative action has occurred, the Conseil d'Etat has the important function of annulling such action or repairing the damage, if it is illegal. This is the work of the Conseil in its judicial capacity.

6

THE JUDICIAL FUNCTION OF THE CONSEIL D'ETAT SINCE 1872: I

THE existence in France of a separate jurisdiction for litigation between the individual and the state is the culmination of an historical evolution which, as we have seen, has its roots in the *ancien régime*. The *Conseil du roi* of the *ancien régime* had certain judicial functions and the king could at any time, by means of *évocations*, remove a case from the sovereign courts to the *Conseil du roi* on the ground that the interests of the crown were involved. However, in spite of this, the *Parlements* constantly interfered in the administration of the country and hampered the work of the *Intendants*. The *Parlements* interfered with reforms and programs of public works and they often called administrators before them to explain or defend their actions. For example, the opposition to the financial reforms of Turgot and Necker was led by the *Parlements*.[1] As a result of these interferences the *Parlements* were viewed with suspicion by the Third Estate.

HISTORICAL BACKGROUND FROM THE REVOLUTION TO 1870

The law of August 16–24, 1790, passed under the revolutionary government, contained a provision prohibiting judges from interfering with the administration. This provision, as has been mentioned above, was the result both of a reaction against the meddling of the *Parlements* with the administration and of the theory of the separation of powers of Montesquieu, though Montesquieu did not conceive the separation of powers in quite the fashion applied by the revolutionary government. The separation of the executive and judicial powers in France, as provided for in the law of August 16–24, 1790, is generally called by French legists the "separation of the administrative and judicial authorities." Article 13 of the law states:

The judicial functions are distinct and shall always remain separate from the administrative functions. The judges shall not, under penalty of forfeiture, interfere in any manner whatsoever with the operation of the administrative bodies, nor summon before them administrators on account of their official duties.[2]

The administrator was to be free from any interference by the courts in the performance of his duties. The theory, popularized by Rousseau, that the executive and his agents were putting into effect the legislative "general will," and therefore should not be troubled by the courts, furnished a theoretical basis for the law.

The prohibition against meddling by the courts in the administration was affirmed several times during the Convention and the Directory.[3] It was taken up again by the famous Article 75 of the Constitution of the Year VIII (1799), which provided:

The agents of the government, other than the ministers, cannot be prosecuted for acts related to their official duties except by virtue of a decision of the Conseil d'Etat; in that case the prosecution takes place before the ordinary courts.[4]

The practical effect of these prohibitions was to place the agents of the government in a privileged position. Before 1800, a person injured by an agent of the government had to address the agent himself or his superior for redress. Thus the administration was both judge and party to the act.

After 1800, the injured person could appeal to the Conseil d'Etat and, in 1806, a special committee on adjudication was created within the Conseil d'Etat to expedite these judicial matters. In addition, a Prefect could have removed to the Conseil d'Etat any case on which an ordinary court had already begun to sit. Then the Conseil would decide if the ordinary court or itself was the competent tribunal to try the case. By this means, the Conseil d'Etat was also the judge of its own jurisdiction. The revolutionary and Napoleonic governments had prevented the judges from administering, but they had not prevented the administrators from judging. The character of the Conseil under the Consulate, Empire, and Restoration was more that of a branch of the executive department than a court. All decisions of the Conseil d'Etat needed the signature of the Emperor or the King to become effective. The members of the Conseil were also appointed by the executive and held office at his pleasure. It was during the period 1820–30 that the Conseil d'Etat first came to be regarded as a court with a definite jurisdiction. This evolution, however, was not completed until the Third Republic. De Tocqueville wrote in 1836:

I tried to explain to them [Americans] that the Conseil d'Etat is not a judicial body in the ordinary sense of the word, but an administrative body whose members are dependent on the king, so that the king, after having ordered one of his servants, called a prefect, to commit an injustice, can order another of his servants, called a Councilor of State, to prevent the former from being punished.[5]

This statement, though perhaps somewhat exaggerated, gives an excellent idea of how far the evolution of the Conseil d'Etat had progressed towards the ideal of a court.

The separation of the administrative and judicial authorities made it possible for the government to prevent the ordinary courts from judging its acts, because conflicts between the individual and the state or its agents were decided in an administrative court, the highest of which was the Conseil d'Etat. Under Article 75, which remained in effect until 1870, the ordinary courts could not entertain a suit against an agent of the government, except by permission of the Conseil d'Etat. Between 1852 and 1864, of 265 applications made to the Conseil d'Etat to prosecute agents of the government before the ordinary courts, only 34 were granted.[6]

This does not mean that the injured party was without a

remedy. He could apply to the Conseil d'Etat which, in the great majority of cases, tried to see that justice was done. However, the decisions of the Conseil needed the signature of the chief of the executive power, except for a brief period during the Second Republic, to become effective. By this means the government could contravene any embarrassing or controversial decision. Viewed in this light the salient features of administrative law were: (1) the special protection of the agents of the government; and (2) prohibiting review by ordinary courts of acts of agents of the state. Although the system of *droit administratif* during this period (1830-70) might well have lent itself to injustice and arbitrariness, there is no evidence that the abuses were more than occasional.

During the period 1830-70 the Conseil had developed into a court, recognized as being solely competent, along with the lower administrative courts, the Councils of Prefecture, to decide cases in administrative law. "Administrative law" and the "decisions" of the Conseil d'Etat are not synonymous. Though the Conseil d'Etat is the highest administrative court and its growth as a judicial body is directly related to the growth of administrative law, the decisions of the Conseil d'Etat are not the sole source of administrative law.

Other sources of administrative law are legislation and *doctrine*. The Conseil d'Etat, like any other court or administrative agency, is organized and reformed by statute. The administrative jurisdiction itself was a result of statutory acts. Statutes can provide the part of administrative law relating to the powers, organization, and forms of procedure of the Conseil and subordinate administrative courts. In the absence of a statutory provision the lacunae can be filled by jurisprudence. The influence of *doctrine* is harder to trace. It derives from legal writers, e.g. professors of law, systematizing the case law of the Conseil d'Etat and extracting the principles of administrative law from it. *Doctrine* also suggests solutions to legal problems and points the way to further developments or innovations. Its sole authority is the ability of the author to convince. Legal writers in France have played a more influential role than their counterparts in England or the United States.

The criterion which governed the separation of the administrative and judicial authorities until about the end of the nineteenth century was a doctrinal construction. This criterion drew the boundary line of the separation of the authorities between acts of authority (*actes d'autorité*) and acts of management (*actes de gestion*). During the Second Empire the Conseil accepted this doctrinal limitation of its jurisdiction.[7] Acts of authority were those which resulted from the exercise of the authority of the state:

Acts of authority are those in which the administration acts by means of orders, in its quality as depository of a part of the public power (*puissance publique*). They do not have any analogy in private law. . . . Acts of management, on the contrary, are those which are accomplished by administrative agents for the management of the private domain and for the functioning of the administrative services. They take the form of acts resembling those which anyone can perform in the administration of an enterprise or of private property.[8]

An act of management was an act accomplished by an administrative agent, an act analogous to that which any private person might perform in the management of his affairs, such as making contracts, buying or selling, or administering land. An example of an act of authority would be the seizure of a newspaper, or the closing of a factory which was dangerous or unhealthful for the residents of the vicinity. These are actions which cannot be accomplished by a private individual. Acts of authority are accomplished by means of orders given by qualified officials. A prefect, for example, can order a newspaper to be seized or a factory to be closed.[9]

The cases involving acts of authority went to the administrative jurisdiction and those involving acts of management belonged to the competence of the ordinary courts. The high point of the acceptance of this criterion was during the Second Empire. It allowed the Conseil to relieve itself of much routine judicial matter. The doctrine was, however, of civil law inspiration and based on Article 1384 of the *Code Civil*.[10] An exception to this rule was that any prosecution based on an act of management tending to declare the state pecuniarily responsible for damages was to be tried by an administrative court.[11] In the *Rothschild* decision (1855) the Conseil d'Etat declared:

> Only the administrative authority has the power (unless it has been otherwise ordered by a special law) to judge the petitions which tend to make the state a debtor. This principle, proclaimed by the decree of September 26, 1793 . . . has become one of the bases of our public law and a general rule for suits against the state by individuals who claim to be its creditors.[12]

This decision was not accepted gracefully by the ordinary courts, which continued to claim jurisdiction under Article 1384 of the *Code Civil*. The matter was not definitively settled until the *Blanco* decision in 1873.[13]

In addition, there was a series of acts called "acts of state" (*actes de gouvernement*) which escaped the control of both jurisdictions.[14] Until 1875, the freedom of acts of state from any judicial control was justified on political grounds (*mobiles politiques*). In cases such as these, *raison d'état* was invoked and the Conseil d'Etat declared itself incompetent to sit. A treatise on administrative law published in 1856 declared:

> That which distinguishes an act of state is the end proposed by its author. An act which has for its basis the defense of society . . . against its interior or exterior enemies, avowed or hidden, present or future, is an act of state.[15]

From this vague definition it is easy to see that the theory of acts of state was capable of allowing the most flagrant governmental arbitrariness under cover of political reasons.

In 1852 the government seized the property of the Orleans family. A petition was brought by the Prince d'Orleans and other members of the family before the Tribunal of the Seine, an ordinary judicial body, on April 12, 1852. On April 15 the Prefect of the Seine issued a *déclinatoire de compétence*, a legal form which forces a court to declare whether or not it is competent. On April 23 the judicial tribunal declared itself competent on the ground that a question of property was involved, the protection of private property having long been a traditional function of the judicial courts. On April 28 the Prefect had the case removed to the Conseil d'Etat. The Conseil decided on June 18: "The decree of January 22, 1852, is a political and governmental act of which the execution and consequences cannot be submitted to the judicial authority." [16] According to this decision neither the ordinary court nor the Conseil d'Etat was competent to try the suit against the government for the return of the Orleans property.

During the Second Empire another classic decision, the *Duc d'Aumale et Michel Lévy* decision, affirmed the doctrine of *mobile politique* in acts of state. Copies of a book, the *Histoire des princes de Condé*, written by the Duc d'Aumale, were seized from their publisher by the Prefect of Police. The author and publisher petitioned the Conseil d'Etat claiming that the act of the Prefect was *ultra vires*. The decision of the Conseil d'Etat stated:

The measure by which the Prefect of Police prescribed, on January 19, 1863, the seizure of said copies, and the decision of the minister of the interior on June 18, 1866, which confirmed the measure are *political acts which are not of a nature to be referred to us*, for *ultra vires*, in our Conseil d'Etat.[17]

Other categories of acts of state, which escaped judicial control, were diplomatic acts and the convocation and dissolution of the legislative assemblies by the executive.

THE TRANSFORMATION OF THE JUDICIAL FUNCTION

On September 19, 1870, after the deposition of Napoleon III, with the German armies marching on Paris, the famous Article 75 [18] was repealed by the Government of National Defense. The practical effect of the repeal was that the judicial courts for a time (until 1873) began to judge civil servants for acts related to their official duties. Meanwhile, the temporary Conseil d'Etat set up in 1870 had little time in which to perform its judicial functions. By the law of May 24, 1872, which reorganized the Conseil d'Etat, a Tribunal of Conflicts was established. The Tribunal of Conflicts was composed of an equal number of members from both the Conseil d'Etat and the Court of Cassation and was presided over by the minister of justice. The Tribunal of Conflicts was set up to decide conflicts of competence between the two jurisdictions.

The first important test of the theory of separation of authorities, which was to decide definitively the future effect of the repeal of Article 75, was the *Blanco* decision of the Tribunal of Conflicts. This decision is the keystone of modern French administrative law. Agnès Blanco, five years old, was injured on a public thoroughfare by a wagon belonging to the state and pushed by the employees of the state tobacco factory in Bordeaux. Her father, invoking Articles 1382, 1383, and 1384 of the *Code Civil*, brought suit for damages against the state and the workers in a civil court. The Prefect of the Department of the Gironde had the conflict removed to the Tribunal of Conflicts. The decision was rendered after the Minister of Justice, Dufaure, broke the tie between the two jurisdictions by voting with the Councilors of State, whose thesis was that the administrative jurisdiction was competent. The decision, which was in agreement with the conclusions of the Government Commissioner, David, stated:

The responsibility which can devolve on the state for damages caused to an individual by the fault of persons that it employs in the public service, cannot be regulated by the principles which are established in the *Code Civil* for the relations of individuals to individuals; this responsibility is neither general nor absolute; it has its special rules which vary according to the needs of the service and the necessity to conciliate the rights of the state with private rights; thus, . . . the administrative authority is alone competent to try them.[19]

It has been noted before that during the Second Empire all actions tending to declare the state a debtor were tried by the administrative jurisdiction. In this respect, the *Blanco* decision was analogous to the *Rothschild* decision of 1855, but whereas the latter was based on the decree of September 26, 1793, concerning the authority capable of declaring the state liable,[20] the law of 1793 was rejected in the *Blanco* decision. The new basis, suggested by the Government Commissioner, David, and incorporated into the decision, was the criterion of public service, the affairs of which, by nature, belong to the competence of the administrative courts. This was a revolutionary doctrine, and if interpreted logically would have meant the abandonment of the doctrine of acts of authority and acts of management, which in turn would have meant that the administrative courts would be competent for all cases arising from acts of management of a public service.[21]

However, the *Blanco* decision was not immediately followed by the abandonment of the distinction between acts of authority and acts of management. In 1887, Edouard Laferrière, then Vice-President of the Conseil d'Etat, was able to write in his *Traité de la juridiction administrative*, one of the landmarks in the systematization of French administrative law, that "the adjudication of acts of the public power [acts of authority] is administrative by its nature, that of acts of management is only administrative by virtue of a law." [22] The administrative courts, according to Laferrière, were competent in cases involving acts of management only when a legislative disposition gave them jurisdiction, with one important exception. This exception stems from the rule of the *Blanco* decision. Only an administrative court could try a suit tending to declare the state liable.[23]

The rule of the *Blanco* decision applied only to the state; until the beginning of the twentieth century the civil courts tried suits for damages against departments and communes. But with the *Terrier* (1903) and subsequent cases, the rule was applied to departments and communes. In 1900 a departmental council voted to give a bounty of 25 centimes for each snake killed in the department and to this end voted a credit of two hundred francs. The credit was quickly exhausted and the Prefect paid an additional 1,566 francs from the credit of Unforeseen Expenses of the departmental budget. Beyond this he refused to pay. A certain Terrier and three other snakekillers claimed payment for 2,473 snakes. They applied to the Council of Prefecture and were informed by the bailiff that the Council of Prefecture was not competent to try the suit. Then Terrier applied directly to the Conseil d'Etat.[24] In spite of the irregularity of the petition—no decision had been officially made by the Council of Prefecture, hence an appeal was logically impossible—the Conseil d'Etat declared itself competent on the ground that the refusal of the Prefect to pay gave rise to a conflict which the Conseil d'Etat was qualified to judge. In his conclusions, the Government Commissioner, Romieu, pointed out that the department had, in fact, created a public service, that of snakekilling. The Government Commissioner went on to say that any conflict arising from the functioning of a public service belonged by nature to the administrative courts:

All that concerns the organization and functioning of the public services . . . general or local . . . constitutes an administrative operation, which is, *by its nature*, in the domain of the administrative jurisdiction.[25]

If the Conseil had accepted the theory of acts of authority and acts of management, the civil courts would have been competent because this was an act of management. Romieu, in his conclusions, explicitly rejected the theory of acts of authority and acts of management. The distinction, in spite of its apparent simplicity, was unwieldy because most administrative acts contained elements of both acts of authority and acts of management.

Romieu, however, proposed one exception, recognized in subsequent jurisprudence, to the rule that litigation arising from the functioning of a public service should be tried by the administrative jurisdiction. This exception was in cases where a public service, for its convenience, chose to act as a private person and thereby voluntarily placed itself under private law (*gestion privé*).[26] Litigation arising from such eventualities was to be tried in the civil courts.

After the *Terrier* decision, it remained to be seen if the Tribunal of Conflicts would accept the lead of the Conseil d'Etat. The Conseil d'Etat has an advantage over the ordinary courts. If an ordinary court sits on a case which the prefect thinks belongs to the administrative jurisdiction, he can have the case removed to the Tribunal of Conflicts; if, on the other hand, the Conseil d'Etat declares itself competent to try a case, there is no machinery by which the case can be removed from the Conseil d'Etat to the Tribunal of Conflicts. Thus, the innovation of the *Terrier* decision could not be definitive unless approved by the Tribunal of Conflicts. The Tribunal of Conflicts in the *Feutry* decision (1908) confirmed the view which the Conseil d'Etat had laid down in the *Terrier* decision.

The main facts of the Feutry case are as follows. At Clermont on the night of September 2, 1906, a dangerous madman escaped from an asylum of the Department of the Oise.[27] Two nights later he set fire to the barn of a certain Feutry, who brought suit for 3,000 francs damages against the Department of the Oise before the civil court of Clermont on the ground that it was a lack of precaution and surveillance which had made the madman's undetected escape possible. The suit was based on Articles 1382–84 of the *Code Civil*. The civil court of Clermont condemned the department to 2,370 francs of damages. The department appealed the decision at the Court of Amiens, and while this court was in the process of considering the appeal, the Prefect of the Oise had the case removed to the Tribunal of Conflicts. In his brilliant conclusions before the Tribunal, the Government Commissioner, Georges Teissier, argued that the competence should be administrative in cases involving the public services of departments and communes, as it was in cases against the state:

> It seems *a priori* that one cannot conceive the possibility of a difference between the situation of the departments or of the communes and that of the state. The public power is one; the character of its acts or of its operations does not change following the territorial importance of the administration which acts. The acts accomplished by the representatives or agents have the same nature, whatever be the extent of the district where these agents act.[28]

Teissier also pointed out that the reasons this type of case had formerly been left to the ordinary jurisdiction no longer existed in view of the development of the role of the Conseil d'Etat.

As in the *Blanco* decision, the vote of the Tribunal ended in a deadlock, and the tie was broken by the Minister of Justice (Briand), who voted in favor of the administrative jurisdiction. In 1908 the Tribunal of Conflicts extended the rule to communes by the *De Fonscolombe* decision.[29] This completed the abandonment of the old theory of acts of authority and acts of management.[30] The new theory of public service had definitively replaced it. In principle, all conflicts arising from the functioning or malfunctioning of a public service were to be tried in administrative courts, with two important exceptions. One is when a law pronounces that the competence is civil, the other when the public service employs the methods of private law (*gestion privée*),[31] as, for example, when it buys furniture or voluntarily makes a civil law contract, thus placing itself under the ordinary jurisdiction. The evolution of the theory of public service considerably enlarged the jurisdiction of the Conseil d'Etat.

The new line of demarcation between the two jurisdictions concerns only suits against the public authorities, and not against individuals. What happens when an employee of a public service is the defendant in a suit? Which jurisdiction is competent? Before the repeal in 1870 of Article 75 of the Constitution of the Year VIII, the ordinary courts could not adjudicate an action brought against a civil servant for a fault related to his official duties without the authorization of the Conseil d'Etat. After the repeal, for a time the civil courts tried suits against public servants for acts related to their duties. The effect of the repeal of Article 75 was nullified by the *Pelletier* decision in 1873. During the war, General de Ladmirault, acting under martial law (*état de siège*), ordered the seizure of the copies of a newspaper published by Pelletier. The latter brought suit for damages and for the restitution of the newspapers in a civil court against the general and other public officials. The case was removed to the Tribunal of Conflicts, which ruled that the suit belonged to the administrative jurisdiction. This decision fixed the practical significance of the repeal of Article 75 as merely abolishing the requirement of the Conseil d'Etat's authorization for the trial of civil servants by the ordinary courts "within the limits of their competence." [32] But, the decision continued, the repeal of Article 75 did not "extend the limits of their jurisdiction" [33] to make all acts by agents of the government liable to review in the ordinary courts. The act of General de Ladmirault was an administrative act belonging to the jurisdiction of the Conseil d'Etat.

In this and subsequent decisions, the line of demarcation between the two jurisdictions was to be determined by whether the damaging act was the result of a "service-connected fault" (*faute de service*) or a "personal fault" (*faute personnelle*). These categories were mutually exclusive, the former belonging to the administrative jurisdiction and the latter to the ordinary jurisdiction. In 1887, Laferrière, then a Government Commissioner, defined these concepts in his conclusions to the *Laumonnier-Carriol* case (1878) before the Tribunal of Conflicts.[34] Laferrière's definitions were elaborated by another famous Government Commissioner, Teissier, in his conclusions for the important *Feutry* case, as follows.

A personal fault . . . is one which shows a man's weaknesses, passions, or imprudences. The personal character of the agent must be revealed by faults of common law, by a *voie de fait* for example; then the fault is imputable to the civil servant and not to his function. The act loses its administrative character and is no longer outside the competence of the ordinary courts. To employ the expression so characteristic of our old authors, a personal fault is one which implies the malevolence of the agent. But if the damaging act is impersonal, if it is an erroneous, faulty, unintelligent, or negligent exercise of the function, if—to employ the expression of your decisions—it does not detach itself from the exercise of the function, if, in other words, it results from a defective organization, or a malfunctioning, or a malexecution of a service, one is confronted by a purely administrative fault.[35]

The conceptions of personal fault and service-connected fault are entirely case law constructions. The definition of these conceptions given by the various legal writers has varied widely.[36] In the twentieth century, the tendency has been to reduce the content of personal fault by requiring that the act must be the result of bad faith or malice on the part of the agent. However, in its main lines, the definition of Teissier is exact.

The *Pelletier* decision and the subsequent development of the concepts of personal fault and service-connected fault confirmed the separation of the administrative and the ordinary jurisdiction in France. An ordinary court could not interfere with the operation of the administration. All cases arising from the operation of the administration (public service) were within the jurisdiction of the administrative courts. The rule of the *Blanco* decision and its extension in the twentieth century by the *Feutry* decision protected the administration itself from interference by the ordinary courts. The *Pelletier* decision and the conception of service-connected fault gave the administrator himself the same protection. Substantially then, in spite of the repeal of Article 75 in 1870, the administration and its agents maintained their privileged position.

In the Third Republic, developments in the Conseil d'Etat made the maintenance of the two separate jurisdictions more palatable to its critics than it had been during the early part of the nineteenth century. The legislative reform of the Conseil d'Etat by the law of 1872 and the case law developments of the Conseil itself caused the liberal opposition, which took its arguments from English law, gradually to disappear. The Conseil came to be considered as a court instead of an adjunct of the administration. One long step toward the curbing of abuse was made when the law of 1872 gave the Conseil the final power of decision. Before 1872, the decisions of the Conseil, to become effective, needed the signature of the chief of the executive power, thus underlining the administrative nature of its adjudications.

In 1889, with the *Cadot* decision, the doctrine of minister-judge was abandoned,[37] a step which completed the "judicialization" of the Conseil d'Etat. The *Cadot* decision marked the culmination of a long development to destroy the theory of the minister-judge.[38] Before this decision the Conseil d'Etat was considered exclusively as a court of appeal, either from the inferior administrative courts or from a minister. Cases where none of the inferior administrative courts was competent were taken to the minister for decision. The decision of the minister was considered to be a regular judicial decision, and respected as such by both orders of jurisdiction. Even though the decisions of the minister were susceptible to appeal before the Conseil d'Etat, the criticism was that the minister was both judge and party to the act. The active administration had judicial powers.

In the *Cadot* decision the Conseil rejected the idea that the decisions of the minister were other than administrative acts, without judicial implications. The petition of Cadot was received directly by the Conseil, without an intermediate decision of the Ministry of Interior. As a result of the *Cadot* decision, cases for which the inferior administrative courts were not competent but which belonged to the administrative jurisdiction could be carried directly to the Conseil d'Etat without the intervention of the minister.[39] If the injured party asked the minister for relief, any action on the part of the minister was an administrative act. By this decision the Conseil d'Etat established definitively the separation of the active administration from the organs of administrative justice.[40]

Another example of the progress of the Conseil toward a more liberal position was the development of the jurisprudence concerning acts of state. The *Prince de Orléans* decision (1852) and the *Duc d'Aumale* decision (1867) during the Second Empire, discussed above, illustrate the broad scope which could be covered by an act of state. In fact, all political regimes before 1870 had employed the theory of acts of state to cover political acts which were often illegal. An act of state was identified by its political motive (*mobile politique*).

In 1873 Prince Napoleon Bonaparte was removed from the list of general army officers. The petition of the prince to the minister of war requesting his reinstatement was refused, after which the prince appealed to the Conseil d'Etat. Before the Conseil d'Etat, the minister contended that the act removing the prince from the army was a political act, an act of state, and thereby escaped review by either jurisdiction. The Conseil d'Etat, in accordance with the conclusions of the Government Commissioner, David, refused to follow the argument of the minister and declared itself competent to judge the case.[41]

The Tribunal of Conflicts followed the lead of the Conseil d'Etat in the *Marquigny* decision (1880), rejecting the contention of the minister that the act expelling nonauthorized congregations was an act of state, and that neither jurisdiction was competent. The Tribunal ruled that the act was an administrative act and that the Conseil d'Etat was competent.[42]

In 1887, in the *Duc d'Aumale et Prince Murat* decision, the Conseil d'Etat affirmed its position once more by rejecting the theory of an act of state based on a political motive.[43] Henceforth, an act of state was to be characterized by its nature and not by its political motivation. This was a reversal of the jurisprudence of the *Prince d'Orléans* (1852) and the *Duc d'Aumale* (1867) decisions. Laferrière in his *Traité de la juridiction administrative* criticized the earlier jurisprudence as going too far:

"It tied itself too exclusively to the intentions, to the political motives of these acts, and not enough to their proper nature which must be the genuine criterion of competence." [44] Thereafter the number of acts of state escaping judicial control was reduced. Since that time the main categories of acts of state have been the acts which concern the relations between the executive and the legislature, such as dissolution, and diplomatic acts, such as treaties.[45]

THE PLEA OF *Ultra Vires*

Petitions received by the Conseil d'Etat can be classified under two general groups: (1) pleas of *ultra vires*, and (2) *recours de pleine juridiction*. Most of the latter group are actions for damages under the law of public liability, which will be taken up in the next chapter.

The plea of *ultra vires* (*recours pour excès de pouvoir*) is the most important means of insuring administrative legality in France. It is a type of remedy unique to French administrative law. The development of this remedy into the important instrument it has become in the twentieth century is mainly the work of the Conseil d'Etat.[46]

Article 9 of the law of May 24, 1872 stated:

The Conseil d'Etat adjudicates pleas of *ultra vires* directed against the acts of the various administrative authorities.

This provision was repeated in Article 32 of the ordinance of July 31, 1945. But at the beginning of the Third Republic this petition still retained some of the semi-administrative aspects it had during the Second Empire. Until 1889, when the theory of the minister-judge was definitively abandoned, the petitioner applied first to the minister and appealed only to the Conseil d'Etat if he had not received satisfaction from the minister. The inferior administrative courts, the Councils of Prefecture, were not competent until 1954 to entertain this type of petition, and are still not competent for all of them. With the abandonment of the theory of the minister-judge, the Conseil became a court of original jurisdiction (*juge de droit commun*) for this type of petition, though in 1953 the Administrative Tribunals were made courts of original jurisdiction for many of these petitions. This petition was developed along lines to give satisfaction to both the administration and the individual. The administration was protected from undue interference by the courts because only the highest administrative court was competent and the judgment was made by a body of men who knew and understood the problems of administration. The effectiveness of the petition and its nominal cost in protecting the individual from the effects of an illegal administrative act assured the respect of citizens. Until the First World War, judgments were also relatively swift.

The procedure of the Conseil d'Etat is very different from that of a regular judicial court. But before we review the mechanism of the petition, we should consider the question of what acts can be challenged. In this matter the field is very broad. A petition is theoretically possible against any administrative act, except acts of state, the decisions of judicial authorities, and acts of the administration in its capacity as manager of the public domain.[47] The last-mentioned exception falls traditionally within the competence of the civil courts. Contracts are also excluded because they are between the administration and another party and could not be annulled without affecting the position of the party contracting with the administration.

Certain conditions, however, must be fulfilled. The act attacked for annulment must, of course, emanate from a French administrative authority: national, departmental, or municipal. The act attacked must be annullable—that is, one could not attack the demolition of his property by the administration by means of the plea of *ultra vires*, but he could bring an action for indemnity. The act must injure the petitioner and he must have a direct and personal interest in its annulment. The content of what constitutes direct and personal interest has been greatly extended in the twentieth century. In the latter half of the nineteenth century the interest justifying a petition tended to be confined to the property rights of an individual, or a civil servant's title to a post, or a citizen's defense of his civil rights. Only in the last decade of the nineteenth century did the Conseil d'Etat begin accepting petitions from collectivities, e.g., companies, in defense of their commercial rights.[48]

In the early part of the twentieth century the idea of interest underwent a rapid extension. The first of a long series of decisions broadening the idea of interest was the *Casanova* decision in 1901.[49] The municipal council of Olmeto, in Corsica, voted in 1897 to hire a doctor to give free medical care to rich and poor alike. For this end they voted a credit of 2,000 francs. There were already two other doctors practicing in the town. Either of these doctors would have had sufficient interest to attack the decision of the municipal council. But the Conseil extended the conditions of admissibility by allowing that one Casanova, a taxpayer, had sufficient interest to attack the decision of the municipal council.

In 1911 the principle was extended to the department in the *Richemond* decision.[50] In this decision the interest of a taxpayer was deemed sufficient by the Conseil d'Etat to attack a decision of the General Council of Seine-et-Oise which provided for free railroad transportation for each of the Council's members. The Conseil has always refused, however, to extend the principle and recognize the interest of a taxpayer as being sufficient to attack an expenditure of the central government.[51]

A voter has the right to attack the decision of a departmental council modifying an electoral district (*Chabot* decision, 1903).[52] A candidate competing for an appointment to an administrative post can attack the findings of a jury or the appointment for illegality. If the appointment injures the interest of a person already in the public service, then that person can attack the appointment as illegal.[53] The idea of interest was even extended to moral interest. After the law on the separation of church and state in 1905, the Conseil d'Etat was deluged with cases of priests attacking the regulations of anti-clerical mayors regulating the ringing of church bells. The Conseil decided that the priests had a moral interest in attacking such decisions.[54]

The Conseil admitted throughout the Third Republic the right of municipal and departmental councils to attack decisions of prefects in relation to the council. In certain cases the interest of a resident has been recognized.[55] In Bordeaux, a company ceased the operation of a streetcar line in a certain district of the town. The residents of the district, led by the Dean of the Faculty of Law at Bordeaux, Léon Duguit, formed a union to defend their right to streetcar service. The Conseil d'Etat in 1906 accepted the petition from this union, judging that the defense of the rights of a district was of sufficient interest to justify receiving the petition.[56] In effect, the application of the idea of direct and personal interest has been very generous, especially since the turn of the century.

The petition is made by the petitioner on stamped paper, and either mailed or delivered to the bureau of the Conseil d'Etat, or since 1953 to the bureau of an Administrative Tribunal. The petitioner explains why he wishes the alleged illegal act to be annulled and he encloses a copy of the act. The services of a lawyer have not been required since 1864, but the petitioner may be represented by a lawyer if he wishes. If the administration refuses to give him a copy of the act under attack, the petitioner can enclose the receipt from a registered letter sent to the administration. The silence of the administration during a period of four months is equivalent to rejection.

The *délai*, or period of time in which the act is subject to attack, is two months. Until the law of April 13, 1900, it had been three months. However, the Conseil has shown itself very liberal in calculating the time limit. An application to a higher official than the author of the act to have it annulled or revised (*recours hiérarchique*) interrupts the time limit, but the petition must be registered within two months after the decision of the higher official if satisfaction is not received. Also the appeal to the higher official must be made within two months after the original decision. Until 1917 an appeal to the author of the act to change or annul it (*recours gracieux*) did not extend the time limit. Since 1917 an appeal to the author of the act interrupts the time limit. The time limit is also extended if the petitioner has applied to a court that was not competent to hear the case. In the case of the implicit rejection by the administration by a silence of four months, the time limit is calculated from the end of the four months. If the decision is published or the petitioner is informed of the decision in writing, the time limit runs from the date of publication or the receipt of notification. The Conseil has not admitted petitions against decisions that were published but did not come to the knowledge of the petitioner until after the expiration of the time limit. However, if the decision is damaging, the petitioner can institute another type of action than the plea of annulment for *ultra vires*.

During the nineteenth cetury the Conseil refused to receive a plea of *ultra vires* if another judicial remedy was available (*recours parallèle*). However in 1912, with the *Lafage* decision,[57] this jurisprudence was liberalized. In this case the other remedy was that of an action for damages for which the Conseil d'Etat was itself competent; the Conseil accepted the plea of *ultra vires* in spite of the fact that another remedy was open because the other remedy was also of the competence of the Conseil. The Conseil has recently accepted petitions when the other remedy was not so effective as the plea of *ultra vires*. However, the Conseil has been cautious where the parallel remedy was in a civil court.

The costs for this type of petition are slight and are paid only if the petition is rejected. In 1958 the cost to the petitioner in case of rejection of his petition was 5,500 francs, or approximately eleven dollars.

The Conseil d'Etat will not accept a plea of *ultra vires* against laws on the ground that they are unconstitutional. The remedy is only open against administrative acts. Until 1907, pleas of *ultra vires* were not admissible against regulations of public administration. The abandonment at the end of the nineteenth century of the theory that regulations of public administration were made by virtue of a delegation of the legislative power helped pave the way for them to be considered as ordinary administrative acts. Curiously enough the Conseil subjected regulations of public administration to its control without abandoning the theory of delegation. The Conseil stated in the *Compagnies du Chemin de fer de l'Est et autres* decision (1907):

> The Head of the State issues a regulation of public administration by virtue of a legislative delegation. This delegation permits the government to exercise in full the powers that have been conferred on it by the legislator. In this particular case, the regulations do not escape, because they emanate from an administrative authority, the petition provided for in article 9 [of the law of 1872].
> Therefore, the Conseil d'Etat, sitting as a court, can examine the content of the regulation and decide if its provisions are within the limit of the delegation.[58]

The position of the Conseil d'Etat in considering a regulation of public administration to be a delegation of the legislative power and at the same time an administrative act was contradictory. Eventually the Conseil dropped the idea of delegation.[59] From 1907 on, the Conseil admitted pleas of *ultra vires* against regulations of public administration. This development was entirely a jurisprudential construction, an example of how, step by step, the Conseil extended its jurisdiction.

A similar evolution took place in respect to colonial decrees issued by the President of the Republic. Until 1931 these colonial degrees were considered a delegation of the legislative power. The Conseil d'Etat in the *Maurel et autres* decision brought this preceding jurisprudence to an end.[60] Colonial decrees were thereafter considered as administrative acts.

If the conditions of admissibility described above have been fulfilled, the Conseil examines the act in detail. The petition is never against the author of the act but against the act itself. Also, the responsibility of the petitioner is never at issue. Thus, the procedure is rather impersonal. The sole result of this petition, if successful, is the annulment of the act. The Conseil cannot change the act or make it conform to legal criteria. It is the duty of the administration to do that. The petition always charges that the act is illegal.

There are four grounds on which the Conseil may annul an act [61] (*moyens d'annulation*) for *ultra vires*. They are: (1) lack of authority (*incompétence*), (2) failure to observe procedures required by law (*vice de forme*), (3) abuse of power (*détournement de pouvoir*), and (4) violation of the law (*violation de la loi*). These grounds are mainly case law constructions of the Conseil, aided by doctrine (the writings of legal scholars). In the early part of the nineteenth century the petition was based on a law of 1790 which provided that complaints against the administrative authorities should be carried to the king as the head of the administration.[62] This illustrates the early administrative conception of the petition. Based on this law the four grounds of annulment existed in some form or another in 1872, developed mainly during the Second Empire. The grounds of lack of authority and failure to observe procedures required by law were the most highly developed; the others existed in embryo.

An act can be annulled for lack of authority because the power to make the decision lies outside the authority of the agent. It can be a usurpation of power, that is, the act might lie outside the power of the administration and properly belong to the legislative or judicial authorities. Or, if not made by a legal administrative authority, it is nonexistent. If the decision of an inferior official rightfully should have been made by his superior, the act is liable to annulment even if it was made with the approval, prior or subsequent, of the superior official. Also liable to annulment is the act of a superior which infringes the authority of an inferior administrative agent, or which belongs to another administrative department. The decision of an agent who refuses to act, on the ground that he is not authorized, is liable to annulment.

When the administrative authority omits the legal formalities required, the act can be annulled for failure to observe procedures required by law. In principle, the omission of a formality brings about the annulment of the act, but the Conseil has allowed attenuations—for the most part the product of common sense. If the formality is nonsubstantial, that is, if the omitted formality could have no possible effect on the decision itself, then the Conseil may refuse to annul the act. Aside from this minor exception, the adherence to formalities is required. For example, the Conseil will annul a regulation of public administration if the Conseil d'Etat, in its administrative capacity, was not consulted. In disciplinary matters the Conseil will annul the decision dismissing an administrative agent if he has not been notified of the charges against him. However, even in this latter case, there is an example of the Conseil refusing to annul a decision dismissing an agent of suspected loyalty during the First World War, who was not notified of the charges against him. The discretionary powers of the Conseil are large and take into account extraordinary circumstances.

Abuse of power results when the administrative agent uses his powers for an end other than that for which the powers exist. Granted that the agent is qualified to make the decision, that he had observed the legal formalities, and that his act violated no rule of law, the act may still be annulled for abuse of power if it can be proved that the act was taken out of personal animosity, for political or religious reasons, or for reasons of personal gain. Even if the act is in the public interest, if it does not conform to the intentions of the legislator in granting the power, it may be annulled. This ground for annulment leaves a wide degree of discretion to the judge. During the Second Empire this ground was employed only exceptionally. It has been employed increasingly since the turn of the century, but the Conseil has always been circumspect in using it. The Conseil always assumes that the powers were employed for a legitimate legal end, unless it is otherwise proved. The proof must be contained in the dossier submitted to the Conseil. Thus if the personal motives of the official are not obvious, the act will probably escape annulment.

For example, in 1905 the Conseil annulled for abuse of power a decision of the minister of war excluding a certain Lespinasse from competing for a grain contract, not because of any lack in his professional capacity, but because the minister disapproved of Lespinasse's religious and political beliefs.[63] Another example is the *Carville* decision of 1896, when the Conseil d'Etat annulled the regulation of a mayor of a municipality which required that all livestock be slaughtered in a municipal slaughterhouse. The purpose of the measure was neither for sanitation nor to assure the quality of the meat, but to increase the revenue of the city and favor local commerce.[64]

The fourth ground of annulment is violation of the law. The word law is taken in its broadest sense—a constitutional law, a law, a regulation, or a decree. To call it, as some authors do, the violation of a rule of law (*règle de droit*) instead of law (*loi*) is more exact. The violation of a rule of law also includes the violation of a general principle of public law or custom which is not necessarily written, such as equality before the law of all persons, the equality of all persons using a public service, or until recently, the liberty of commerce. Until the twentieth century the Conseil would allow this petition only if a vested right (*droit acquis*), a right already possessed, were injured, but this qualification was dropped. For example, if a prefect refused to approve a decision of a General Council of a department on the ground that the decision was illegal, no recourse would have been open in the nineteenth century because until the approbation of the prefect was given, the General Council possessed no vested right. But if the approbation had been given by the prefect and was subsequently withdrawn, then a petition would have been open because a vested right had been violated, assuming of course that the prefect was in error as to his powers.[65]

No petition is admissible against a law on the ground that it violates a constitutional provision, and until 1907 the Conseil did not admit petitions against regulations of public administration on the ground that a law had been violated. Violation of the law includes the misapplication of a law owing to an error in the interpretation of the law. Some laws and regulations provide that certain necessary conditions be fulfilled before a decision can be made. If these conditions are not fulfilled because the administrator did not grasp the situation correctly, then the decision is annullable on the ground of an error of fact (*erreur de fait*). Some authors consider an error of fact as a fifth ground of annulment, but the majority have assimilated it to violation of the law. The violation of judicial decisions is considered a violation of the law. Negatively, the decision of an agent who, erroneously, refuses to make a decision on the ground that he lacks authority, is annullable.

The plea of *ultra vires* can only result in the annulment of the act and this annulment operates *erga omnes*. Not only is the act annulled for the plaintiff, but also, if the scope of the act is general, for everyone. The petition for annulment is not an action between parties, but an action directed against the act alleged to be illegal. After the petition has been filed the petitioner has nothing more to do. There are no opposing lawyers, witnesses, or cross-examinations usually associated with a court of law. The case progresses on the basis of written reports. Optionally, the petitioner may employ a lawyer to put the petition in correct legal form and to submit observations, in writing, to the unit of the judicial section judging the petition.

The dossier of the petition is studied by a reporter of the subsection sitting on the case. The reporter, either a Maître des Requêtes or an auditor, then submits his report giving the facts of the case. He also presents a solution and drafts a proposed decision. The matter is then deliberated in a subsection. On the basis of the report and the discussion in the subsection examining the case, the Government Commissioner, usually a Maître des Requêtes, presents his conclusions proposing the decision, either for annulment of the act or the rejection of the petition (assuming it has satisfied the conditions of admissibility). The Government Commissioner does not present the state's case; his conclusions are based on what he believes the law to be.[66] After the Government Commissioner has presented his conclusions, the members of the unit judging the case, usually two subsections united, discuss the case and vote on the decision. The decision is made by majority vote. It often happens that the conclusions of the Government Commissioner, who does not vote, are rejected. The petitioner is then notified of the Conseil's decision. In the event that his petition fails, he must pay a small sum.

The decision proper is in a traditional form. First there is the *visas*, an analysis of all the applicable laws, regulations, and documents in the dossier. This is followed by the *considérants* or *motifs*, which set out in abbreviated form the salient features of the case and contain the reasons for the Conseil's decision. At the end of the decision is a sentence or two signifying the rejection or the admissibility of the petition (*dispositif*). The decision is normally one or two paragraphs in length and usually incomprehensible without reference to the conclusions of the Government Commissioner.

When an act is annulled, the Conseil does not stipulate the consequences of the annulment; for example, if a public servant is illegally dismissed and the Conseil annuls the act of dismissal, the decision of the Conseil does not state what the administration must do to rectify its illegal act. Once the act is annulled the petitioner can again address the administration for redress. The administration must make a new decision in line with the decision of the Conseil d'Etat. If the administration persists in its refusal, the petitioner may file a new petition of *ultra vires*, this time for violation of a judicial decision. A petition for indemnity is also usually open. There are several examples where the administration continued to make new decisions having the same effect as fast as the Conseil annulled them.[67] To enforce respect for the decisions of the Conseil, it has been suggested that the refusal of an agent to adhere to a judicial decision should make him personally liable, the sanction to be applied by the ordinary judicial tribunals, which have jurisdiction over cases of personal fault.[68] As yet there have been no examples of this.

Although not strictly petitions of *ultra vires*, there are two other types of petitions which should be mentioned as part of the judicial function of the Conseil d'Etat. These are the petition for cassation and the petition for appreciation of validity on "prejudical questions." The petition for cassation is an appeal against the decision of another administrative court whose decision is "in last resort," such as the Court of Accounts (*Cour des Comptes*). In the appeal for cassation, the Conseil determines only if the law has been applied correctly and if the court was competent. It does not review the facts of the case. If the Conseil annuls the decision, the case is returned to the same court, assuming that it was the competent one, to be retried.

Because of the two orders of jurisdiction there often arises a question in a case before a civil court as to whether a certain administrative act is illegal. If the judge declares, rightly or wrongly, that he is incompetent to pass on the legality of the act, and if it is necessary to determine the legality of this administrative act before the case at hand can be decided, then the civil court recesses until such time as one of the interested parties has petitioned the Conseil d'Etat on the legality of the act. This is called a "petition for appreciation of validity" on a "prejudical question." The Conseil, in contrast to the plea of *ultra vires*, does not annul the act but merely declares that it is "tainted with illegality." The Conseil does not draw the conclusions resulting from the illegality of the act. This is the function of a civil court.

In summary, the advantages of the petition of *ultra vires* are its inexpensiveness, its relative simplicity, and the broad protection it offers to the citizen from arbitrary administrative action. However, there are limiting factors on its effectiveness. The decision of the administration is always executory and the petition of *ultra vires* can only redress a wrong; it cannot prevent the wrong from being committed.[69] That the French administration be free from any interference in the execution of its tasks has been a jealously guarded principle since the Revolution.

Another limiting factor is the slowness of the decision, resulting from an overcrowded docket, which has been rather persistent since about 1910. There is a multitude of examples of decisions which have come five or six years after the petition was filed. In some of the cases the relief afforded was largely illusory. The shortness of the period of delay in which the petition may be filed—two months—is also a limiting factor. However, in many cases where the plea of *ultra vires* is ineffective, especially where pecuniary interests have been damaged, the action for damages under the law of public liability is available to give relief.

7

THE JUDICIAL FUNCTION OF THE CONSEIL D'ETAT SINCE 1872: II

THE action for damages under the law of public liability, which includes most of the actions falling under *pleine juridiction*, differs from the plea of *ultra vires* both in the object of the plaint and the type of relief afforded. The powers of the judge are also different. The plea of *ultra vires* is an extraordinary petition, the action being directed against the act, while the action for damages under the law of public liability is an ordinary petition, being, in the judicial sense, a contest between parties. In the plea of *ultra vires* the petitioner, having a direct and personal interest, asks for the annulment of an illegal act, and, if the petition is successful, the annulment is *erga omnes*. In the action for damages, the plaintiff, on the basis of having been the victim of a damaging act, claims from the administration a restitution or a sum of money, for himself alone. The action for damages under the law of public liability is a suit between the plaintiff on the one hand and the administration on the other.

The Conseil in the plea of *ultra vires* passes on the legality of the act. In the action for damages under the law of public liability the Conseil determines the position of an individual in relation to an allegedly damaging act. The former is directed against the legality of the act; the latter to secure some kind of indemnification. In the action for damages, the judge can reform the act, that is, he can substitute his own decision for that of the administration and condemn the administration to pay damages, hence the significance of the French title *pleine juridiction*.

For the action for damages under the law of public liability the services of a lawyer are required,[1] whereas the services of a lawyer are only optional in the plea of *ultra vires*.[2] The requirements covering the time limit are also more liberal; the action can be initiated at any time up to thirty years after the damaging act. The injured party can address the administration for redress at any time within thirty years,[3] but if the administration refuses to give satisfaction the injured party must address the Conseil within two months after being notified of the administration's decision.

In the action for damages under the law of public liability the Conseil was sometimes a court of original jurisdiction (first instance) and sometimes a court of appeal from the lower administrative courts such as the Administrative Tribunals, formerly called Councils of Prefecture, the Administrative Tribunal of Alsace-Lorraine, and the administrative councils of the French colonies. In any case, the Conseil d'Etat is the court of final jurisdiction. The cases which had to be taken to the inferior administrative courts in first instance were determined by law. Since the reform of 1953, the Administrative Tribunals are courts of first instance for this type of action, with few exceptions.

THE ACTION FOR DAMAGES UNDER THE LAW OF
PUBLIC LIABILITY [4]

The most important types of petitions coming under *pleine juridiction* are: (1) petitions relative to the responsibility of the public power, and (2) petitions relative to administrative contracts. Besides these, there are the petitions relative to direct taxation (an individual might claim himself to be overassessed), petitions regarding the salary and pensions of public employees, and petitions challenging elections. The most significant and numerous of the cases falling under *pleine juridiction* are actions for damages. During the Third Republic the jurisdiction of the Conseil over the matters grouped under *pleine juridiction* was increased at the expense of the ordinary judicial courts. Also, important qualitative developments took place, particularly in the field of responsibility.

To appreciate the extent of the change, the state of the action for damages under the law of public liability at the beginning of the Third Republic must be examined.[5] Under the terms of the *Blanco* decision, decided by the Tribunal of Conflicts in 1873, the responsibility of the state was "neither general nor absolute" and it belonged to the Conseil d'Etat alone to ascertain this responsibility. The rule of the *Blanco* decision applied only to the state and not to the communes and departments where the ordinary courts continued to receive actions for damages based on Articles 1382-86 of the *Code Civil*. Until the *Blanco* decision, the theory, developed by civil law specialists, of acts of authority and acts of management held full sway. Even though the *Blanco* decision laid down the principle that only the Conseil d'Etat could determine the responsibility of the state for an act of management, it was not until the early part of the twentieth century that the logic of this decision was applied to the departments and communes.

Until the twentieth century, the Conseil recognized the responsibility of the public service only for faults which were the result of an act of management. Acts of authority, an exercising of sovereignty, were not reparable.[6] That the state was irresponsible for its acts of authority was a survival of the idea that the king could do no wrong. Of course, the administration could repair a damage if it so desired, even for an act of authority. In any case, the injured party had first to address the minister for a decision before he could appeal to the Conseil d'Etat.

Responsibility was closely tied to the concept of fault; in principle, there could be no responsibility without a fault. An exception to this was damages caused by public works, where the State would indemnify the injured party even if no fault had been committed by the administration, but this responsibility was based on a law which dated back to 1806. The Council of Prefecture was a court of first instance for this type of case with an appeal possible to the Conseil d'Etat. However, this responsibility had its limits. The damage had to be material and direct; no responsibility could result from the nonexecution or tardy execution of public works.

Of all the petitions, that of responsibility has undergone the greatest transformation, and that transformation was accomplished mainly by jurisprudence. The jurisprudence of the Conseil in matters of responsibility was extended to the departments and the communes at the expense of the civil courts. The extension took place in the first decade of the twentieth century— the important decisions being those of *Terrier* (1903) and *Feutry* (1908), both discussed above,[7] which established the principle that the administrative courts were competent to try actions in responsibility against the departments. With the *de Fonscolombe* decision (1908),[8] the Tribunal of Conflicts extended the principle to the communes.

This extension of the jurisprudence of the Conseil d'Etat in matters of responsibility was coincident with the abandonment by the Conseil of the criteria of acts of authority and acts of management in matters of responsibility. In principle, the responsibility for acts of management had been recognized throughout the Third Republic, but the Conseil had, until the eve of the twentieth century, declared that the state was irresponsible for acts of authority. *Les torts du souverain ne se réparent pas* was the proverbial expression in French law.

In 1886, a certain Lepreux, while on his way to the railroad station of the commune of Maisons-Alfort, walking on a public thoroughfare, was wounded in the eye as a result of the firing of a cannon in connection with a fair that was being held in the commune. Two policemen were present.

Lepreux brought suit against the state for indemnification,

charging malfunctioning of service, the surveillance of the police having been inadequate. Action was brought against the state and not against the commune because the police were under the control of the Prefect of Police of the Department of the Seine. The decision of the Conseil rendered on January 13, 1899, stated:

> Concerning the request for indemnity of *sieur* Lepreux:—To maintain that the state owes him reparation for prejudice which was caused to him as the result of an accident occurring on August 8, 1886, in the commune of Maisons-Alfort, *sieur* Lepreux bases [his suit] on the fact that the authors of this incident were under insufficient surveillance by the police, which is exercised in the communes of the Department of the Seine under the authority of the Prefect of Police;—but . . . it is a principle that the state is not, as the public power (*puissance publique*), . . . responsible for the negligence of its agents.[9]

The demand for indemnity of Lepreux was rejected because "it is a principle that the state is not, as the public power, . . . responsible for the negligence of its agents." This is to say that the state is not responsible for its acts of authority. The commentary of Maurice Hauriou on the *Lepreux* decision is interesting.[10] Hauriou, highly critical of the decision, showed a desire, common among legal writers of the period, to extend the area of responsibility of the state. Hauriou proposed, in sum, a radical extension in the interpretation of acts of management (for which the state was responsible) at the expense of acts of authority (for which the state was not responsible). Concluding his commentary on the decision, Hauriou suggested that the decision should have read:

> It is true that the public power is irresponsible when it acts by way of acts of authority; it is also true that, when it acts by way of management, it is responsible for accidents which are occasioned by the irregular functioning of the organized services.[11]

Thus for Hauriou there would have taken place a condemnation of the state to pay an indemnity for an insufficient functioning of the police. Hauriou did not propose the abandonment of the theory of acts of authority, only its diminution. The method by which the Conseil d'Etat finally chose to extend the responsibility of the state was not that suggested by Hauriou. The boldness of the solution must have been a surprise even to the warmest advocates of the extension of state liability.

The circumstances surrounding the Greco case were almost the same as those of the Lepreux case. In Tunisia, one Tomaso Greco was wounded in his own home by a shot fired, apparently by a gendarme, at an escaped bull. The Conseil d'Etat in the *Greco* decision [12] (1905), just six years after the *Lepreux* decision, refused to allow an indemnity, but not for the same reason as in the *Lepreux* decision. In the latter decision the Conseil refused to grant an indemnity because the state was irresponsible for its acts of authority. In the *Greco* decision, an indemnity was refused because there was no proof that a gendarme had fired the shot which wounded Greco. The decision stated:

It is not clear from the inquiry that the shot which wounded *sieur* Greco was fired by the gendarme Mayringe, nor that the accident which the plaintiff has suffered can be attributed to a fault of the public service, for which the state would be responsible.[13]

In this decision there is no mention of the irresponsibility of the state. The responsibility of the state is, on the contrary, implicitly recognized in the phrase: "a fault of the public service for which the state would be responsible." Only the circumstances surrounding the accident prevented the Conseil from granting the indemnity. The *Greco* decision marked the abandonment of the distinction between acts of authority and acts of management in matters of responsibility. The criterion which replaced it was "fault of the public service." Only a week after the *Greco* decision, in the *Auxerre* decision,[14] the Conseil granted an indemnity for a "fault of the public service."

The concept of fault of the public service was extended to include eventualities where the public service had not functioned, a fault of omission (*Département de la Dordogne* decision, 1907).[15] In 1919, the Conseil decided that the tardy execution of a public service also constituted a fault of service (*Brunet* decision).[16] For a fault of the public service to engender responsibility, the fault must have a certain gravity; any fault or imprudence on the part of the victim diminishes the responsibility of the state, department, or commune, or may quash it entirely. It can be said that a grave illegality always engenders responsibility, especially if there has been a violation of a law or judicial decision, or an "abuse of power."

The Conseil d'Etat has also extended the principle of responsibility to certain cases where there has been no fault committed, a responsibility for risk. Responsibility for risk arises from a fortuitous or unexpected eventuality. The cause is usually unknown. This is to be distinguished from a *force majeure*, where the cause is known and for which the Conseil does not recognize responsibility. Examples of *force majeure* are earthquakes, cyclones, and foreign invasions. The first application of the theory of risk was the *Cames* decision of 1895.[17] Cames, a worker in an arsenal run by the Ministry of War, was the victim of an accident which deprived him permanently of the use of his left hand. The Ministry of War granted Cames the sum of 2,000 francs, an indemnity which the Ministry claimed was purely gratuitous because no fault could be shown on the part of the administration. Cames brought a suit before the Conseil d'Etat for an increase in the amount of the indemnity. The Conseil judged that the accident was not due to a fault on the part of the state nor was the accident imputable "either to the negligence or to the imprudence" of Cames. The Conseil went on to grant Cames the sum of 600 francs a year for life. This constituted a recognition of professional risk (*risque professionnel*), which preceded by several years the recognition of such responsibility by statute.

Another application of the risk theory is the *Regnault-Desroziers* decision (1919).[18] In 1916, the explosion of some grenades stored in a fort caused damage to the neighboring property of one Regnault-Desroziers. The cause of the explosion was unknown. The Conseil granted the plaintiff indemnification for the damage. The decision stated that the "risks were of a nature, . . . to engage, independently of any fault, the responsibility of the state." [19] In this case the Conseil recognized a risk due to the proximity of the property of Regnault-Desroziers to the fort.

In the *Colas* decision of 1920,[20] the Conseil decided that the explosion of powder on the warship *Liberté* brought about the responsibility of the state in regard to third parties because the large amount of powder on the ship prior to maneuvers, constituted an "exceptional risk." Just eight years before in a case of almost the same circumstances, the Conseil had denied damages. This was the *Ambrosini* decision of 1912.[21] An explosion on board the warship *Iéna* caused the death of an eighteen-months-old child on the street several blocks from the docks. This the Conseil d'Etat treated as a case of *force majeure*. The only difference invoked in the decisions between the two cases appears to be the exceptional amount of powder that the *Liberté* was carrying in view of forthcoming maneuvers. However, there were eight years between the two judgments, and the *Colas* decision can be regarded as a step forward in the extension of the responsibility of the state.[22] The law of May 3, 1921, relating to war damages thwarted the jurisprudence of the Conseil in the case of exceptional risk due to proximity (*voisinage*), but when the law lapsed in 1945, the Conseil resumed its jurisprudence in this field.[23] Since 1945 the theory of risk has been still further extended in police measures because the employment of "arms or engines comports exceptional risks." [24]

Another development in the petition for indemnity is the granting of an indemnity where there has been a personal fault on the part of the agent and not a service-connected fault. Normally a personal fault—a case which would be tried before a civil court—would engender the personal liability of the agent. However, because the resources of the agent are usually insufficient to repair the damage, the Conseil d'Etat has accepted the theory of the cumulation of responsibilities (*cumul des responsibilités*). Before this development in the Conseil's jurisprudence, which took place in the second decade of the twentieth century, the concepts of personal fault and service-connected fault were considered mutually exclusive: the existence of one precluded the pecuniary liability of the other.

In the cumulation of responsibilities one can distinguish two hypotheses: (1) where there is a double fault, both a personal fault and a service-connected fault, there is a cumulation of responsibilities; (2) where there is a cumulation for only a single fault which is mixed. The first hypothesis is illustrated by the *Anguet* decision of 1911,[25] which was the inaugural decision for cumulation of responsibility for a double fault.

A certain Anguet, attempting to leave a post office, found the exit locked although it was before the regulation hour of closing. He was invited to use an exit reserved for employees. While leaving by this exit he was physically assaulted by two employees of the post office and his leg was broken. Here there were two faults: a service-connected fault—the public exit was locked before closing time; and a personal fault—the assault by the two employees. A civil court had found the two employees guilty of assault, but the suit for indemnity was brought by Anguet before the Conseil d'Etat, which granted an indemnity.

The *Lemonnier* decision of 1918 [26] is an example of a mixed fault, that is, the coexistence of a service-connected fault and a personal fault in the same act. It was the custom of the commune of Rocquecourbe (Tarn Department) to organize an annual fair. One of the diversions of the fair was to shoot at rabbits, ducks, or chickens, which were attached to wooden blocks and allowed to float down a river. Early in the afternoon the mayor of the commune had been warned that the firing made it dangerous for strollers on the public thoroughfare on the opposite side of the river. The mayor did not order the firing to cease but merely changed its direction so as to minimize the possibility of an accident. Later in the afternoon the wife of one Lemonnier was grievously wounded.

Lemonnier started actions before both orders of jurisdiction. The Tribunal of Toulouse, a civil court, held that the mayor was personally responsible and ordered him to pay 12,000 francs in damages. While the mayor was appealing the decision of the Court of Toulouse before the Court of Cassation, the Conseil d'Etat rendered its decision. In his remarkable conclusions, the Government Commissioner, Léon Blum, pointed out that it was not in the province of the Conseil d'Etat to decide if there had been a personal fault, or to question the judgment of the Court of Toulouse, but it was up to the Conseil to decide if there had been a service-connected fault. To determine if there was to be a cumulation of responsibility, Blum proposed the following criterion:

However, if it [the personal fault] has been committed in the service, or on the occasion of the service, if the means and the instruments of the fault have been placed at the disposition of the guilty only by the operation of the service, if, in a word, the service has conditioned the accomplishment of the fault or the production of its damageable consequences *vis-a-vis* a determined individual, the administrative judge will be able to say: the fault detaches itself from the service, an affair for the civil courts to decide, but the service does not detach itself from the fault.[27]

The Conseil admitted the responsibility of the commune and ordered it to pay 12,000 francs in damages, with the reservation that the indemnity not be duplicated. In other words one could not be indemnified twice for the same cause. However, the decision of the Conseil did not go so far as to incorporate all the implications of Blum's definition. With reservations, it admitted responsibility only for faults committed in the service. Nevertheless the *Lemonnier* decision greatly widened the concept of responsibility by what might be called an extension of the concept of the service-connected fault. Subsequent jurisprudence has extended it still further. In 1949 the Conseil granted indemnities for automobile accidents occurring outside the service in cases where an agent used an automobile, belonging to the civil or military service, for his personal ends.[28]

Paralleling the development of responsibility is the jurisprudence of the Conseil concerning administrative contracts. Although a civil contract is essentially an agreement between equals, the administration is clearly predominant in an administrative contract. For example, the administration can terminate an administrative contract at its convenience, subject to the payment of an indemnity for work already completed, or for commitments of the contracting party with third parties. The main types of administrative contracts are those between the administration and entrepreneurs for public works, or with entrepreneurs for the purpose of a continuing public service such as gas, electricity, or the water supply. The conventions that were negotiated periodically with companies for the building and operation of railroads were administrative contracts. The concessions of the state for mining and the supplying of the administration with the goods that it needs for its operation—e.g., army contracts for war matériel or food—are also administrative contracts. Not all contracts between the administration and a private person or company are administrative contracts. The administration may voluntarily place itself under ordinary civil contracts (*gestion privée*).

An administrative contract is usually awarded after competitive bidding, though this is not always true. There is always a set of conditions (*cahier des charges*) setting out the requirements for the execution of the contract by both the administration and the contracting party. The litigation relating to administrative contracts arises from the alleged nonobservance of the conditions of the contract on the part of the administration. For example, the administration might have unilaterally revoked a contract with an entrepreneur for the building of a road or bridge and refused to indemnify him for the expense he had already incurred prior to the revocation of the contract. On the basis of this administrative decision the entrepreneur can appeal to the administrative courts for indemnification. Or the administration might give rise to the action by adding or changing certain requirements in the contract, which it has a right to do. The action for an indemnity would result only if the administration refused to indemnify the contracting party for the losses resulting from the changes.

In some cases, depending on the nature of the administrative contract, the Councils of Prefecture were courts of original jurisdiction with appeal to the Conseil d'Etat, such as petitions concerning mining concessions. In other cases, such as the conventions passed with the railroads, the action was carried directly to the Conseil d'Etat. Since the reform of 1953, the Administrative Tribunals are courts of original jurisdiction for all administrative contracts.

The development of the jurisprudence governing administrative contracts is analogous to that which took place in responsibility. First, the administrative jurisdiction has been extended at the expense of the civil jurisdiction; second, a liberalization and extension of the jurisprudence of the Conseil so as to give greater rights to the parties contracting with the public authorities, national or local, has taken place.

Until the eve of the twentieth century the civil courts were recognized as the competent jurisdiction for suits arising from administrative contracts for the communes and departments. The development extending the jurisdiction of the Conseil to this area culminated with the *Thérond* decision in 1910.[29] A contract between Thérond and the city of Montpellier gave Thérond a monopoly in the disposal of unclaimed dead dogs and also of all diseased dogs of which the owner was known. The city failed to execute its part of the contract in assuring Thérond of a monopoly, thereby causing a prejudice to Thérond. In fact the contract could not be executed because it violated the principle of freedom of commerce. The decision of the Conseil granted Thérond an indemnity for the financial loss he suffered by the failure to execute the contract. More important was the part of the decision where the Conseil ruled itself competent to judge the case:

> The city of Montpellier acted in view of the hygiene and the security of the population . . . to insure a public service; thus the difficulties which can result from the nonexecution or the faulty execution of this service are, in the absence of a [legislative] text attributing the competence to another jurisdiction, of the competence of the Conseil d'Etat.[30]

This decision marked also the extension of the concept of "public service" to the realm of administrative contracts to which the local public authorities were a party. Since the turn of the century the principles applied by the Conseil d'Etat to contracts are more liberal than those applied by the civil courts under the *Code Civil*. An example of this is the "theory of unforeseen circumstances" (*théorie d'imprévision*) developed by the Conseil.

The application of the theory of unforeseen circumstances is well illustrated by the *Compagnie du gaz de Bordeaux* decision in 1916.[31] A contract between the city of Bordeaux and a gas company provided that the company furnish gas to the residents of the city at a certain price per square meter calculated on the price of coal per ton. The maximum price that the company was allowed to charge for gas under contract was based on the price of coal at 28 francs per ton. Before 1914 the price of coal was approximately 15 francs a ton, but shortages, caused by the war, resulted in a rise in the price of coal; at the end of 1915 coal was more than 70 francs a ton. The city of Bordeaux refused to allow the company to raise the price of gas above that called for in the contract. It was thus only a matter of time before the company would be forced into bankruptcy. The case came before the Conseil d'Etat, which ruled that the company was entitled to an indemnity.

The circumstances causing the unforeseen and extraordinary rise in the price of coal were independent of the contracting parties. It was necessary for the company, as a public service, to continue to supply gas to the users which it could not do if forced into bankruptcy. In view of this the Conseil rendered a decision on the lines of equity. Such a suit in a civil court would probably have failed. This was the first application of the theory of unforeseen circumstances. The application of this jurisprudence has been frequent in France since 1916 owing to the recurring devaluation of the currency since the First World War. In the application of the theory, the Conseil examines the position of the company as a whole. The administration is under no obligation to insure the company a profit; the indemnity is granted to insure the continuance of operation of the company. Part of the loss is expected to be borne by the company, but, in practice, the largest part of the loss is borne by the administration.[32]

Another type of *recours de pleine juridiction* is that regarding pensions and salaries of public servants or military personnel. For these cases the Conseil was directly competent. This action, however, requires the services of a lawyer and court costs are substantial, unlike the plea of *ultra vires*, in which the costs are nominal. This has the effect of discouraging suits to recover relatively small sums. In pension and salary cases, however, the plea of *ultra vires* is now possible. Some of the petitions that would have belonged to *pleine juridiction* in the early years of the Third Republic, such as pension cases, have been partly absorbed by the plea of *ultra vires*.

The petition concerning elections is unlike other petitions in the category of *pleine juridiction* in that it is gratuitous, and no lawyer is necessary. The time limit is brief, usually five days, and the cases are usually judged within three months. This petition resembles the plea of *ultra vires* more than it does other petitions of *pleine juridiction*, and at least one text considers it as *ultra vires*.[33] Elections to the national legislative assemblies are excluded as these assemblies are themselves judges of the regularity of the election of their members. Included are the elections of communal and departmental councils, mayors, and other locally elected officials. The competence for election cases since the laws of 1926 and 1934 [34] has been given to the Councils of Prefecture with the right of appeal to the Conseil d'Etat. Before 1926, the Conseil was alone competent. In the case of an irregularity, the election can be annulled. The petition can be filed by any elector living in the district where the alleged irregularity occurred.

THE POLITICAL AND SOCIAL SIGNIFICANCE OF THE JURISPRUDENCE OF THE CONSEIL D'ETAT

Most of the credit is due the Conseil d'Etat, acting as a court, for the three great developments in administrative adjudication that have been discussed above: (1) the development of the plea of *ultra vires*, (2) the recognition of the pecuniary responsibility of the state for its sovereign acts, and (3) the application of the principle of equity to administrative contracts. In the main these developments were the accomplishments of the jurisprudence of the Conseil d'Etat and took place independently of legislative enactments. In many cases legislative enactments later confirmed what the jurisprudence of the Conseil had already established. These developments served to extinguish the liberal opposition against the administrative jurisdiction that was found in the National Assembly in 1872. From its somewhat inauspicious beginning in the early years of the Third Republic, the Conseil erected a series of legal safeguards that gave the French citizen after the turn of the century a protection in some respects superior to that enjoyed in Anglo-American countries.

As has been said above, the Conseil d'Etat has no right to pass on the constitutionality of laws. At one time it seemed to some observers that the Conseil would assume such a right. Some legal writers urged the Conseil to do so. However, the Conseil failed to do so and now the opportunity for such a development has passed. Given the French legal structure such a development might have been impossible anyway. In his commentary on the *Winkell et Rosier* decision of 1909,[35] Hauriou remarked:

The power of the judge to refuse to enforce laws that he deems unconstitutional exists in Anglo-Saxon countries. There are no good reasons why it should not be established here. The Conseil d'Etat, judge of the legality of acts of the administration, is in a position to inquire into the constitutionality of laws that it is asked to apply.[36]

For Hauriou the *Winkell et Rosier* decisions could only be explained on the ground that Article 65 of the law of April 22, 1905, was unconstitutional in case of a strike. However, neither the conclusions of the Government Commissioner Tardieu, nor the decision, invoked any such reasons in rejecting the petitions of Winkell and Rosier.[37]

Winkell and Rosier were two employees of the post office who were discharged from their employment by decree of an under-secretary of state at the time of a strike of postal, telephone, and telegraph employees. The two men involved petitioned the Conseil to annul the decree of the under-secretary on the grounds of the violation of Article 65 of the law of April 22, 1905. This article provided that no civil servant could suffer such disciplinary action without being informed of the nature of the charges and the identity of his accusers. The case of a strike was not foreseen in the provisions of the law of 1905.

In rejecting the petitions of Winkell and Rosier, the Conseil utilized the argument that in striking the employees voluntarily ruptured their contract with the administration and placed themselves outside the protection of Article 65. The act of striking deprived them of their status as civil servants. This reasoning appeared insufficient to Hauriou. To him the decisions could only be explained by the unconstitutionality of Article 65 in time of a strike:

Our decisions are explained juridically only by the thesis of the unconstitutionality of the law of 1905, as applied in time of strike; as such, they will be invoked as a precedent in favor of the unconstitutionality of laws.[38]

In this Hauriou was to be disappointed, because there was no subsequent development along these lines. It should be noted that there are some differences between the type of constitutional control Hauriou thought feasible and the doctrine of judicial review as understood in the United States.[39] Because of the brevity of the French constitutional texts of the Third Republic, Hauriou thought that it would have been difficult to erect a broad system of review. To get around this he proposed to distinguish between ordinary and fundamental laws. The legislator himself could do so, or the courts. In the case where a fundamental law was in conflict with an ordinary law the ordinary law would be inapplicable. It would not be inapplicable *erga omnes*, as in the United States, which would result in nullity, but only within the limits of the specific case. For the case under discussion this would mean specifically in time of strike; in normal times the law would still be applicable. Apart from the practical technical difficulties which would arise from the suggestion to make a distinction between fundamental and ordinary law, it is difficult to see how such a step could have been taken without the consent of parliament. In France this consent is almost impossible to conceive because of the zeal with which the chambers have guarded their prerogatives. Public opinion in France might not have supported the Conseil in such an attempt, and in the absence of a favorable public reception, the parliament would have been free to apply sanctions against this "pernicious doctrine." [40]

However, there is an interesting exception to the concept of the non-reviewability of laws. This was on the occasion of the *Heyriès* decision in 1922,[41] which is the only example of the Conseil overriding a law by an appeal to the higher authority of constitutional law. Heyriès was a civilian employee of the Ministry of War, who was dismissed during the war because of suspected loyalty. The dismissal took place without Heyriès being informed of the charges against him as provided for by Article 65 of the law of April 22, 1905. A decree, issued at the beginning of the war, of September 10, 1914, had suspended the application of Article 65 for the duration of the war. At the time there were many decrees which either suspended the application of or modified laws. This was a patent illegality and the parliament by the law of March 30, 1915, retroactively validated a whole host of them. Probably due to a clerk's oversight, the decree of September 10, 1914, was not listed. This oversight placed the Conseil in the difficult position of having to justify how a decree could repeal the provisions of a law.[42] In its decision, the Conseil resorted to two reasons: (1) the legitimate defense of the state in time of war, and (2) the terms of Article 3 of the constitutional law of February 25, 1875.[43] The decision stated:

By Article 3 of the constitutional law of February 25, 1875, the President of the Republic is placed at the head of the French administration and is responsible for insuring the execution of the laws. . . . It was within his [the President's] power on September 10, 1914, at which date was issued the decree of which the legality is contested, to decide that the communication to every civil servant of his dossier preliminary to any disciplinary sanction, prescribed by Article 65 of the law of April 22, 1905, was of a nature during the period of hostilities to prevent, in a great number of cases, disciplinary action from being exercised and to hinder the functioning of the various services necessary to the national life; because of the conditions under which the public services actually operated at this period, it was his [the President's] duty to take the indispensable measures for the execution of the public services placed under his authority.[44]

The Conseil validated the decree suspending, in time of war, the provisions of a law by an appeal to a higher law—the constitutional law. It was a recognition that the normal regime of legality can be suspended in time of war by reason of necessity—a recognition of an emergency power. This case served as a precedent for a number of cases, arising from the Second World War, in which the Conseil suspended the operation of a law because of "exceptional circumstances." In these later cases, however, the suspension was not justified by reference to the Constitution.

The Conseil may interpret the Constitution in the absence of a law, as it did in the *Dehaene* decision of 1950.[45] In this decision the Conseil ruled on the right to strike guaranteed in the preamble of the Constitution of 1946, as applied to employees of the public service. The Constitution guaranteed the right to strike "within the cadre of the laws which regulate it [this right]."[46] The parliament, however, had passed no laws regulating the right to strike of employees of the public service. It was the Conseil d'Etat itself which finally decided the meaning of the clause. During the Third Republic the Conseil by the *Winkell* decision of 1909, discussed above, ruled that by striking, the striker lost his right to the guarantees accorded to civil servants. This jurisprudence was firmly maintained throughout the Third Republic. A civil servant could be dismissed merely for engaging in a strike. In the *Dehaene* decision of 1950, the Conseil d'Etat ruled:

It [the power] belongs to the government, responsible for the functioning of the public services, to fix, under the control of the courts ... the nature and extent of the limitations which must be added to this right [to strike] as to all other rights, with a view toward avoiding a usage, abusive or contrary to the necessities of public order.[47]

Actually, under the Fourth Republic, the striking civil servant is not separated from his guarantees quite so absolutely as he was in the Third. But the necessity for continuity of the public services has, in the jurisprudence of the Conseil d'Etat, taken precedence over the right to strike.[48] The *Dehaene* decision ruled that in the absence of a law on the right of civil servants to strike, the government may place limitations on this right, subject to the control of the Conseil d'Etat. Also, from a constitutional point of view, the *Dehaene* decision recognized this section of the preamble of the Constitution of 1946 as having the same value as the rest of the Constitution.[49] It is difficult to say just what the legal value of the Constitution is. Theoretically, constitutional law is above ordinary law but there is no effective sanction to prevent the parliament from violating the Constitution.

In the absence of legal texts the Conseil is often called upon in its judicial decisions to "say the law." In the *Mogambury* decision of 1892,[50] the Government Commissioner, Jean Romieu, in his conclusions was led to define the powers of the office of under-secretary of state. The rank of under-secretary of state was not defined in any constitutional or ordinary law.

The rules governing the duties and privileges of all civil servants were, under the Third Republic, largely composed of the jurisprudence of the Conseil d'Etat, erected in the absence of a legal text. When, during the Fourth Republic, a law fixing the status of civil servants was passed (the law of October 19, 1946), it was for the most part a codification of the anterior jurisprudence of the Conseil d'Etat.[51]

In spite of its close relations with the government, the Conseil has many times demonstrated its complete independence in judicial matters. In one instance a decision of the Conseil d'Etat led to the fall of a cabinet and the resignation of the President of the Republic. On January 12, 1895, the Conseil rendered a decision[52] concerning the guarantee of interest under the Reynal Convention of 1883 to the railroad companies Paris-Orléans and the Midi. The decision was contrary to the thesis maintained by the Minister of Public Works, Louis Barthou. Because he did not wish to carry on negotiations with the railroad companies under the terms of the decision of the Conseil d'Etat, Barthou resigned two days after the decision. His resignation provoked the resignation of the whole Dupuy cabinet on the 17th, followed by that of the President of the Republic, Casimir-Périer.[53] Barthou's resignation, which set off this surprising chain of events, was not the necessary consequence of a judicial decision against the thesis of the Minister of Public Works, but rather the personal refusal of the minister to accept the consequences.[54] This exceptional example is without parallel, but it illustrates emphatically the independence of the Conseil from governmental pressure in judicial matters.

If the jurisprudence of the Conseil d'Etat is examined for its social content, it becomes apparent that, considered socially the Conseil d'Etat was neither in advance nor far behind the dominant opinion of the time in its attitude toward socialism, freedom of contract, or free enterprise. The jurisprudence on the right to strike of employees of the public service has already been alluded to above from the point of view of its relationship to the position of the Conseil regarding the interpretation of the Constitution. The right of civil servants to form unions was not recognized by the Conseil d'Etat until the Fourth Republic where this right is guaranteed by the preamble of the Constitution and the law of October 19, 1946. This attitude of the Conseil has not, in the twentieth century, always been in accord with that of the government. The government has at times tolerated, at times encouraged, unions of civil servants. In the 1930's, some of the members of these unions were appointed to official consultative commissions in their capacity as representatives of a corporate group. However, the Conseil declared these appointments illegal.[55] This divergence between the attitude of the government and the jurisprudence of the Conseil was ended in 1946 [56] by the Constitution and the law of October 19, 1946.

The attitude of the Conseil d'Etat toward any municipality engaging in a commercial or industrial enterprise, "municipal socialism," as it was called, has been discussed above in relation to the consultative function of the Conseil. In its judicial capacity the Conseil added a sanction to the opinion of the administrative sections. An example of this is the above-mentioned *Casanova* decision of 1901 [57] by which the Conseil annulled the decision of a municipal council which provided for the post of a communal doctor to give free medical service to the inhabitants of the town, at an annual salary of 2,000 francs. There were already two doctors practicing in the town, which caused the Conseil to regard the decision of the municipal council with disfavor. Only five years earlier in the *Bonnardot* decision,[58] the Conseil d'Etat had allowed a similar decision by a municipal council to stand, but in this case there were no other doctors practicing in the town.

In another case involving municipal enterprise, the *Boulangers de Poitiers* decision,[59] the Conseil nullified the decision of the municipal council of Poitiers. The municipal council granted a subsidy of 9,500 francs to a cooperative bakery which undertook to bake and sell bread at less than the market price, thus injuring the business of the town's other bakers. In these decisions regarding "municipal socialism," the Conseil declared the establishment of commercial and industrial enterprise by a municipality illegal, on the basis that it was not expressly allowed by the law of April 5, 1884, concerning municipal organization. Neither was it expressly forbidden, although Article 63 of the law stated that a decision of the municipal council was null if the object of the decision was outside its powers. Still, the Conseil ignored this provision in "exceptional circumstances," as in the *Bonnardot* decision, where private enterprise did not fulfill the needs of the community. Whether or not the Conseil enforced the law of 1884 depended upon whether or not the enterprise of the community was in competition with private enterprise. This is an illustration of the large discretionary powers of the Conseil to give either a broad or a narrow interpretation to the law of 1884 depending on the occasion. Its jurisprudence cannot be said to run counter to the prevailing economic and political philosophy of the time. After the First World War, the decree-laws of November 5 and December 28, 1926, extended the powers of the municipalities in regard to economic matters. The report preceding the latter decree-law stated that the jurisprudence of the Conseil, "despite its evolution, still lags behind actual necessities." [60] The effect of these decree-laws was not very great because they were strictly interpreted by the Conseil.[61]

During the Third Republic the Conseil was opposed to any troubling of the principle of liberty of commerce and freedom of contract, such as the regulation of wages and hours, but its opportunity to meddle in this field was somewhat restricted because most of these matters fell within the province of the civil courts. Before the turn of the century the Conseil annulled several decisions of the municipal council of the city of Paris prescribing minimum wage and hour regulations in contracts with entrepreneurs for public works undertaken by the city.[62] This jurisprudence was ended by the intervention of the so-called Millerand Decrees of August 10, 1899.

Limitations of scope and space prevent the description of other fields where the jurisprudence of the Conseil has played an important role. Some of them may, however, be briefly mentioned. If perhaps the Conseil has lagged a bit behind in its views on social matters, though it has certainly been far in advance of the ordinary judges of the civil jurisdiction, it has encouraged technological progress and has been a hardy defender of civil liberties.[63] When at the turn of the century, technological advances brought about a change from gas to electricity for lighting, many of the cities of France were in a difficult position because of their contracts with gas companies. The Conseil ruled that these contracts were to be interpreted as only giving the gas companies the right of preference to furnish electric lighting. They could not prevent cities from granting concessions to furnish electricity even though the contracts gave the gas companies a monopoly of lighting.

With regard to civil liberties, the Conseil, by its jurisprudence, moderated the conflict between the Catholics and the anti-clericals after the separation of the church and state in France. The jurisprudence on the matter of religious liberties is as important as the laws and decrees on the subject. Since 1944, however, the Conseil has greatly extended its protection of civil liberties by a new and significant jurisprudential creation called the "general principles of law" (*principes généraux du droit*). A member of the Conseil has characterized the "general principles of law" as "without doubt the most singular and audacious of all the jurisprudential constructions of the Conseil d'Etat."[64] This jurisprudence has made great progress in the protection of the liberty and equality of all citizens in cases where there is no statutory guarantee. The area in French public law where no legislative text exists is great,[65] and, until recently, the Conseil was cautious of ruling in instances not covered by a legal text.

One of the leading cases in this new jurisprudence was the *Trompier-Gravier* decision of 1944.[66] The widow Trompier-Gravier was the proprietor of a newstand on one of the boulevards in Paris. Her license to sell newspapers was revoked by the Prefect of the Seine because she tried to extort the sum of 40,000 francs from an employee. The decision of the Prefect of the Seine was annulled because the widow Trompier-Gravier, the object of a quasi-judicial proceeding, had not been given a chance to defend herself or prove the inaccuracy of the facts. Because there had not been a proper hearing, and in the absence of any legal text on the subject, the decision of the Prefect revoking her license was annulled. This annulment goes beyond the ground of "failure to observe procedures required by law" because there was no legal text requiring a hearing. There is, as has been discussed above, a statutory provision requiring the communication of the dossier and a hearing prior to any disciplinary action against civil servants, but newspaper vendors are not civil servants.

The theory of the "general principles of law" has often been invoked in matters of liberty of conscience, non-retroactivity of an administrative act, and the equality of all citizens regardless of their race or religion. This theory was used under the Vichy government, when the Conseil tried, with caution, to lighten the operation of the racial laws by interpreting them loosely.[67] At the end of the German occupation, the Conseil also abated somewhat the policy of dismissal of certain civil servants who had served the Vichy government. This jurisprudence pleased neither the category of civil servants who were allowed to be dismissed nor those resistance leaders who wanted a more thorough "purification." [68]

The foundation of the "general principles of law" is rather general. They can be said to be founded on the Declaration of the Rights of Man of 1789, on rules recognized in civil law, and on rules deduced from the "nature of things." [69] The jurisprudence invoking the "general principles of law" is limited. It cannot overrule a legislative act and can only be applied if the legislator has not expressed a contrary wish.[70] In spite of this limitation, this jurisprudence has been a great stride forward in the judicial role of the Conseil. In the words of a member of the Conseil, Mr. Letourneur: "The theory of the 'general principles of law' even though it doesn't permit unlimited hope . . . , constitutes, nevertheless, the most remarkable jurisprudential construction in recent years and, without doubt, the most 'praetorian' and fruitful in a long time." [71]

It is apparent from the discussion Chapters 6 and 7 that the judicial role of the Conseil has grown considerably since the beginning of the Third Republic. Much of this growth has been owing to increasing governmental intervention in the economic and social spheres. Since the end of the First World War, the increase in the number of cases brought to the Conseil has had the unfortunate result of causing judgments to take so long that there was in many cases a virtual denial of justice. This slowness invariably worked hardship on the parties concerned. One might well say that administrative adjudication has been crushed by its own success. The easy accessibility to the Conseil and the large number of cases for which it was a court of original jurisdiction, until the reform of 1953, had in the end encumbered it. Even with the new reform, it remains doubtful if the Conseil will be able to expedite its cases owing to the vast expansion of the judicial role. The major causes of the expansion—nationalization of industry and state intervention in economic and social affairs—are, in many respects, only beginning in France. The table of statistics in the Appendix amply illustrates the growth of the judicial work of the Conseil.

In a sense, the reform of 1953 is a major landmark which marks the end of an era in the development of the judicial function of the Conseil. Since the *Cadot* decision of 1889, the Conseil has been a court of original jurisdiction for all *ultra vires* cases, but the great growth of the judicial function made it impossible for the Conseil to continue to hear these cases in first instance.

Thus, for the majority of these cases, original jurisdiction was given to the Administrative Tribunals, formerly the interdepartmental Councils of Prefecture. As a result of the reform of 1953 the Conseil, as a court, may be said to have reached adulthood. The majority of its cases now come on appeal from the Administrative Tribunals.

From the above pages, the contributions which the Conseil d'Etat has made to the public life of France become abundantly clear. This body has, indeed, played an important role in attaining one of the fundamental goals in Western civilization—that of assisting in regulating human affairs, within known rules of behavior, equal for all and according to widely accepted principles of justice and ethics. Within the structure of French governmental institutions the Conseil's part has been one of aiding in the functioning of the other branches of public life. It has not, at least in recent times, been tempted to usurp the prerogatives of other political institutions—it has been devoted to performing its designated tasks and performing them well. Of the various services that the Conseil is called upon to render, the most fundamental is that of protecting the French citizen from illegal administrative action. Slowly but steadily the Conseil has helped to build up a body of law and precedent to this end. This development took place, in part, at the expense of the ordinary courts and was consistent with the adoption of the criteria of "public service," under which all cases that pertained to the public service came within the administrative jurisdiction. The criteria of "public service" replaced that of acts of authority and acts of management as the line of demarcation between the two jurisdictions. The result was to add acts of management, which formerly belonged to the ordinary courts, to the Conseil's jurisdiction. In this development the Conseil was aided by the composition of the Tribunal of Conflicts, which allows the minister of justice to cast, as we have seen, the deciding vote in the event of a tie. On several occasions the vote of the minister of justice has been decisive in extending the Conseil's jurisdiction.

Second, the Conseil increased the protection of the citizen against illegal administrative action by the development of the plea of *ultra vires* and the recognition of the liability of the public powers for their sovereign acts. The plea of *ultra vires*, as it exists in France, is a highly original petition, for it enables an injured citizen to obtain the annulment of an act with a minimum of inconvenience and expense. At the same time this petition gives as little offense as possible to the administration, which feels that its interests are better protected by the Conseil d'Etat than they would be if these cases were tried before an ordinary court. Within the administration, civil servants look to the Conseil to guarantee rights pertaining to their employment. At the turn of the century the Conseil, taking another stride forward, recognized that the state was pecuniarily responsible for its sovereign acts. At first, the liability of the state could arise only from fault, but this was later extended, as we have seen, to a liability for risk, independent of fault.

Third, the Conseil has played an important role as technical counselor of the government. Because the Conseil had been one of the leading institutions of the Second Empire, it was in disrepute at the beginning of the Third Republic, and its function as technical counselor was accordingly small. However, in the course of time certain factors helped to alter this situation. With the tremendous growth in the services performed by the modern state, parliament had to delegate an increasing amount of its task to the executive. Modern legislation had to be limited to setting forth general principles, the implementation of which was left to the executive and its auxiliaries. In the formulation of this secondary, or "delegated legislation" as it is called in Britain and the United States, the Conseil has become a highly competent advisor on which the government could call. Furthermore, French "ministerial instability," arising from the difficulty in finding a stable majority in the French parliament, and party factionalism resulting in a growing inability of the leglisature to act, led to the granting of decree-law power to the executive and to calling upon the Conseil to examine the drafts of decree-laws, especially under the Fourth Republic. As we have also seen, since 1945 all government bills have been submitted to the Conseil for examination, a development that has further increased the role of the Conseil as technical counselor.

These developments have not only enabled the Conseil to retain and increase its role as a court and to augment its role as an advisory body, but have given it unequaled prestige among French institutions. Criticism of the Conseil's jurisdiction, which was common during most of the nineteenth century, has disappeared. Today it would be difficult to find an advocate of destroying the administrative jurisdiction.

APPENDIX A. OPINION OF THE CONSEIL D'ETAT OF FEBRUARY 6, 1953, CONCERNING ARTICLE 13 OF THE CONSTITUTION [1]

The Conseil d'Etat:
Convoked by the President of the Council of Ministers on the question: "What is the definition and the exact meaning of the interdiction contained in Article 13 of the Constitution[?] To what extent, explicitly authorized by law, can the government exercise its rule-making power in legislative matters, and as a consequence, abrogate, modify, or replace legal texts by means of regulatory [executive] dispositions [?]"

By the terms of Article 13 of the Constitution of October 27, 1946: "The National Assembly alone votes the law. It cannot delegate this right."

It follows from the debates preceding the adoption of this article, the principle of which was already contained in Article 55 of the draft Constitution drawn up by the first Constituent Assembly, and also from the procedure on the debating and voting of laws contained in Articles 14 and following of the Constitution, that the authors of Article 13 intended to forbid the recourse to decrees issued by virtue of laws of habilitation such as were voted under the Third Republic.

However, the legislator can, in principle, definitively determine the extent of the rule-making power and, toward this end, can decide that certain matters within the competence of the legislative power will enter within the competence of the rule-making power. Decrees issued by this means can modify, abrogate, or replace legislative dispositions, and can be modified themselves by other decrees, until the

[1] *Revue du droit public,* 1953, pp. 170–71.

legislator decides anew to exclude the matters in question from the competence of the rule-making power.

But, certain matters are reserved for legislative acts, either by virtue of dispositions of the Constitution, or by the republican constitutional tradition, stemming notably from the Preamble of the Constitution and the Declaration of the Rights of Man of 1789, whose principles have been reaffirmed by the Preamble. The legislator cannot transfer these matters to the competence of the rule-making power, though the legislator can confine itself to setting forth the main principles and leave the government the task of completing them.

Finally, by virtue of Article 3 of the Constitution, national sovereignty resides in the French people who "exercise it through their deputies in the National Assembly, except for constitutional matters." The extension of the competence of the rule-making power would be contrary to Article 3, if, by its generalness and haziness, it manifested the will of the National Assembly to abandon the exercise of national sovereignty to the government.

APPENDIX B. NUMBER OF CASES DECIDED BY THE CONSEIL D'ETAT, 1852-1958

Period	Average Number of Decisions per Year [1]	Period	Average Number of Decisions per Year [1]
1852–60	983	1914–20	1,930
1861–64	1,174	1920–25	3,375
1872–77	1,347	1925–30	4,749
1878–82	1,643	1930–35	7,112
1883–87	1,730	1935–38	6,442
1893–95 [2]	1,849	1938–46	2,620
1895–1900	2,618	1946–51	4,480
1900–1905	4,407	1951–56	4,478
1905–10	3,708	1956–58	4,681
1910–14	4,207		

[1] The figures to 1887 are from the quinquennial *Compte général des travaux*. Those after 1946 can be found in the annual *Etudes et documents*. The others were supplied to the author by the courtesy of Mlle. Marie Lainé, Secretaire du contentieux au Conseil d'Etat.

[2] Commencing with August 1, 1893, the judicial year runs from August 1 until July 31.

NOTES

JO is used throughout the notes to designate *Journal officiel.*

1. THE PLACE OF THE CONSEIL D'ETAT AMONG FRENCH INSTITUTIONS

1. Alexis de Tocqueville, *Oeuvres complètes,* éd. par J. P. Meyer (Paris, 1951), II, 1, 107–27.
2. Especially the *Conseil privé* of the *Conseil du roi.*
3. In Britain between 1894 and 1913 the annual average of "general" rules and orders was 210 compared with 1,211 for 1950. Sir Cecil Carr, "Delegated Legislation," in *Parliament, a Survey,* ed. by Gilbert Campion, First Baron (London, 1952), pp. 240–41.
4. See Chapter 3 for a description of the consultative councils.
5. The author has been assured by a distinguished Councilor of State that the social background of the new recruits for the Conseil d'Etat is generally the same as under the Third Republic, although now there are a few who have come from a modest background.
6. The Blum government of 1936 is a case in point.
7. On this point see Penfield Roberts, *The Quest for Security* (New York, 1947), p. 49.
8. By means of the so-called "conclusive evidence" clause. See Marguerite A. Sieghart, *Government by Decree* (London, 1950), pp. 130–32, and Bernard Schwartz, *Law and the Executive in Britain* (New York, 1949), pp. 188–96.
9. Charles H. Pouthas, *Démocraties et capitalisme (1848–1860)* (Paris, 1941), p. 164.
10. See Chapter 2 for an account of this dispute.
11. In France the term "delegated legislation" is not used because, in theory, the legislative power cannot be delegated.
12. These forms are defined in Chapter 5.
13. This leaves aside the question of "decree-laws."
14. With the exception of the action of the administrative sections and the Permanent Commission, which sometimes pass on the con-

formity of a bill with the Constitution. However, the government is free to ignore their advice.

15. André Ferrat, *La République à refaire* (Paris, 1945), p. 179. Ferrat's charges against the Conseil are in many instances grossly exaggerated.

16. Frank J. Goodnow, *Comparative Administrative Law* (New York, 1893).

17. Only in the seventh edition of 1908 did Dicey distinguish administrative adjudication, with which he was primarily concerned, as only a part of French administrative law. In an article in the *Law Quarterly Review* in 1901 ("*Droit Administratif* in Modern French Law," XVIII, 302–18), Dicey admitted that many of his judgments on French administrative law were no longer true, but curiously enough, in spite of this admission, the later editions of his book did not reflect how much his views apparently had changed.

18. In 1949 an American professor of administrative law still accepted Dicey's view that French administrative law is incompatible with English rule of law. Schwartz, *Law and the Executive in Britain*, p. 151. See his later *French Administrative Law and the Common Law World* (New York, 1954), pp. 310–11.

19. Dicey implicitly admitted in the seventh edition (1908) that he had been misled by de Tocqueville's view of the Conseil of the Restoration and the Empire.

20. They still do, although their irremovability is tacitly recognized. The power of removal has been exercised only once since 1879, in 1945 during another period of upheaval.

21. For this decision see Chapter 6.

22. Léon Aucoc, *Conférences sur l'Administration et le droit administratif* (3ème éd., Paris, 1885), I, 449.

2. THE STRUCTURE OF THE CONSEIL D'ETAT, 1872–1940

1. Décret du 19 septembre 1870.
2. Rapport de A. Batbie, *JO*, 19 février 1872, pp. 1195–96.
3. *JO*, 19 juin 1871, annexe no. 279, pp. 1453–56.
4. *Ibid.*
5. Of the Constitution of the Year VIII (1799).
6. Constitution du 4 novembre, article 72. For all constitutional texts since the Revolution, see: L. Duguit, H. Monnier, and R. Bonnard, *Les Constitutions et les principales lois politiques de la France depuis 1789* (7ème éd. par Georges Berlia, Paris, 1952).

7. Article 75.
8. Robert Dreyfus, *De M. Thiers à Marcel Proust* (Paris, 1939), p. 145. The members from the left were Limpérani, de Rémusat, Marc Dufraisse, and Bethmont.
9. The reporter (*rapporteur*) in the French parliamentary system draws up the committee report on a bill and defends it before the Assembly.
10. *Cours de droit public et administratif* (3ème éd., Paris, 1869).
11. *JO*, 19 février 1872, p. 1196.
12. [Duc Léonce-Victor de Broglie,] "Les Tribunaux Administratifs," *Revue française* (novembre 1828), pp. 58–132, especially 122 ff.
13. *Recueil des arrêts du Conseil d'Etat, Biens de la Famille d'Orléans*, 18 juin 1852, p. 258.
14. *JO*, 20 février 1872, p. 1224.   15. *Ibid.*
16. *Ibid.*, pp. 1214 ff.   17. *Ibid.*, p. 1220.
18. *Ibid.*   19. *Ibid.*
20. *Ibid.*, p. 1221.
21. *JO*, 24 avril 1872, p. 2725. Of the seven sponsors, five were affiliated with parties on the right and two with parties on the left.
22. *JO*, 30 avril 1872, p. 2871.
23. At this time the royalist sympathies of Thiers were doubted by many of those wishing to restore the monarchy. The membership of republicans, like Dufaure, in his cabinet did nothing to quell their doubts. Even at this time (early in 1872) Thiers was regarded with some favor on the left.
24. *JO*, 2 mai 1872, p. 2929.   25. *Ibid.*, p. 2931.
26. 3 mai 1872, p. 1.
27. *Le Temps*, 3 mai 1872, p. 1; *Journal des débats*, 2 mai 1872, p. 1.
28. 5 mai 1872, p. 1. De Marcère in his *Histoire de la République de 1876 à 1879*, II, *Le Seize Mai et la fin du septennat* (Paris, 1910), 77–78, reports that he, with Francisque Rive, Amable Ricard, and Agénor Bardoux, dined with Thiers early in May. He records Thiers' irritation with the vote and also his decision to resign unless the right of appointment was restored. "One cannot govern with his head in the dust," he reports Thiers as saying.
29. 3 mai 1872, p. 1.
30. *JO*, 24 mai 1872, p. 3462. Author's italics.
31. Duc de Broglie, *Mémoires*, II, *1870–1875* (Paris, 1941), 110. Broglie admitted that to allow the Assembly to elect Councilors of State was contrary to the principle of the Conseil d'Etat itself. Broglie mistakenly referred to the compromise he proposed as increasing

the number of Councilors of State in special service. This was probably owing to a lapse of memory.

32. *Le Temps,* 26 mai 1872, p. 1. Article Three was adopted on May 24 by a vote of 403 to 261.

33. A text of the law can be found in the *JO,* for 24 mai 1872, pp. 3463-64.

34. The duties of the reporter in the Conseil d'Etat are described in Chapter 3.

35. *Compte général des travaux du Conseil d'Etat de 1872 à 1877* (Paris, 1878), p. xxxii.

36. Décret du 21 avril 1913, article 11.

37. *JO,* 24 mai 1872, p. 3463.   38. *Ibid.*

39. Dreyfus, *De M. Thiers à Marcel Proust,* p. 185.

40. *JO,* 26 février 1875, pp. 1468-71.

41. *Ibid.,* p. 1471.

42. The question of why the Assembly voted to elect Councilors of State in 1872 and left the power to the President of the Republic in 1875 was the occasion of a debate, at two meetings of the Société de l'histoire moderne in 1936, between Robert Dreyfus and Daniel Halévy. Dreyfus contended that the change in front was due solely to the fact that Thiers was no longer President of the Republic. Halévy admitted that this was one of the factors but he advanced others as being of equal importance. Halévy contended that liberal opinion unfavorable to the Conseil, especially during the Second Empire, was an important factor in the decision of the Assembly to elect Councilors of State. It was difficult for Halévy to reconcile this view with the overwhelming vote in 1875 in favor of the amendment, so he resorted to the explanation that the amendment was rushed through before the opposition had a chance to coalesce. Halévy admitted that the support given to the amendment by the Left was "inexplicable." He ignored the fact that the Left also supported it in 1872. This "parliamentary trickery" thesis, espoused by Halévy, is based on the outbursts of Raudot, the Duc de la Rochefoucauld-Bissaccia, and the Marquis de Castellane on February 25, 1875. Still, the vote, by roll call, was 467 to 46, the opposition coming wholly from the extreme right. "Trickery" or not, the majority appeared to know what it wanted. *Bulletin de la Société d'histoire moderne,* Nos. 10 and 11 (1936); Halévy, *La République des ducs* (Paris, 1937), pp. 176-81; Dreyfus, *De M. Thiers à Marcel Proust,* pp. 141-209.

43. Joseph Barthélemy and Paul Duez, *Traité de droit constitutionnel* (nouv. éd., Paris, 1933), p. 678.

44. "Rapport au Garde des sceaux, présenté au nom de la Commission d'études pour la réforme du Conseil d'Etat, par M. Henry Puget" (typewritten: Paris, 1945), p. 38, hereafter referred to as "Rapport pour la réforme du Conseil d'Etat."

45. Loi du 7 juillet 1887.

46. A Government Commissioner is a public official attached to the court. He sums up both sides of the case before the judges and suggests what decision should be made. He is not the state's attorney in the American sense; his conclusions are based on what he believes the law is, be it for or against the plaintiff.

47. See Appendix B for statistics.

48. Loi du 26 octobre 1888 and loi du 17 juillet 1900.

49. Loi du 13 avril 1900.   50. *Ibid.*   51. *Ibid.*

52. Loi du 8 avril 1910 and loi du 1er mars 1923.

53. A reaction against these "ministerial wills" (*testaments ministériels*) set in after the fall of the second Briand government in February, 1911, and brought about an attempt to suppress them by the finance law of July 13, 1911. The chief beneficiaries of these "ministerial wills" were the personnel of his cabinet. Not many found places on the Conseil d'Etat because of the limited number of vacancies. Louis Rolland, "La Réaction contre les abus du favoritisme," *Revue du droit public*, XXVIII (1911), 571, 572, and 579.

54. Loi du 13 juillet 1911.

55. *Revue du droit public*, XXXIII (1916), 66.

56. Julien Laferrière, "L'Organisation de la juridiction administrative, Réformes et projets de réforme," *Revue du droit public*, XXXVII (1920), 556.

57. A. Guillois, "L'Organisation de la juridiction administrative: Projets de réforme," *Revue du droit public*, XL (1923), 85n.

58. *Ibid.*, p. 86.

59. Proposition Marin, *JO, Documents parlementaires, Chambre des Députés*, 1920, annexe no. 222. pp. 105–8.

60. Laferrière, "L'Organisation de la juridiction administrative, Réformes et projets de réforme," *Revue du droit public*, XXXVII (1920), 556–57.

61. There was a Council of Prefecture in each department. The various reform bills called for eighteen to twenty-six regional councils to replace them.

62. This type of solution has been proposed several times: see Louis Ricard, *JO, Documents parlementaires, Chambre des Députés*, 1891, annexe no. 1452, pp. 1348–58; Edouard Barthe et Jean Félix,

ibid., 1920, annexe no. 578, p. 486; Emile Bender, *ibid.*, 1925, annexe no. 1469, pp. 512–13.

63. Proposition Marin, *ibid.*, 1920, annexe no. 222, pp. 105–8.

64. The following tabulation shows the fluctuation in membership between 1930 and the outbreak of World War II:

	Counselors of State	Maîtres des Requêtes	Auditors First Class	Auditors Second Class
Law of April 16, 1930	39	43	21	26
Decree-law of May 5, 1934	30	39	20	15
Law of December 31, 1937	36	43	25	25

Since 1945 the upward trend in membership has continued:

	1945	1950	1956
Vice-President	1	1	1
Section Presidents	5	5	5
Counselors of State	42	46	44
Maîtres des Requêtes	45	49	69
Auditors	45	48	52
Totals	138	149	171

3. THE STRUCTURE OF THE CONSEIL D'ETAT SINCE 1940

1. Tony Bouffandeau, "Le Juge de l'excès de pouvoir jusqu'à la Libération du territoire métropolitain," *Conseil d'Etat, Etudes et documents*, No. 1 (Paris, 1947), pp. 23–27.

2. The laws of the Vichy regime were not legislative acts in the strict sense because there were no elected assemblies; the legislative power had been delegated to Marshal Pétain who had the *de facto*, if not *de jure*, exercise of this power.

3. René Cassin, "Introduction," *Conseil d'Etat, Etudes et documents*, No. 1 (Paris, 1947), p. 13.

4. Porché was simply retired on pension. His case was not considered by a committee of *épuration*.

5. "Rapport au Garde des sceaux, présenté au nom de la Commission d'études pour la réforme du Conseil d'Etat, par M. Henry Puget" (typewritten, Paris, 1945), pp. 7–8.

6. *Ibid.*, p. 8.   7. *Ibid.*, p. 25.

8. These members are not to be confused with the Government Commissioners of the judicial section.

9. "Rapport pour la réforme du Conseil d'Etat," p. 29*bis*.

NOTES TO 3: STRUCTURE OF THE CONSEIL SINCE 1940 179

10. André Ferrat, *La République à refaire* (Paris, 1945), p. 180.
11. "Rapport pour la réforme du Conseil d'Etat," p. 39.
12. *Ibid.* 13. *Ibid.*, p. 43.
14. *Le Monde*, 6 février 1952, p. 7.
15. *Le Figaro*, 6 février 1952, p. 1.
16. For example, one of the women choosing the Conseil would have preferred the Ministry of Foreign Affairs but, for a woman, opportunities for advancement there would have been limited. Also, the vacancies in the Inspection of Finance were filled with the eleventh choice; of students ranked twelfth through fifteenth, some may have preferred the Inspection of Finance. The Court of Accounts ran a poor third to the other two corps.
17. The only example is Léon Blum, who presided once in 1947.
18. Because of the heavy load carried by the Section President, the post of Assistant President was created in 1956 to aid him (loi du 4 août 1956).
19. Prior to 1950 there were only eight subsections. A ninth was added in 1950 to judge cases arising from motor-vehicle accidents in which a vehicle of the state was involved (décret du 12 décembre 1950). In 1956 two more subsections were added, bringing the total to eleven. The addition of these two subsections was aimed at expediting the work of the Conseil (loi du 4 août 1956).
20. Georges Cahen-Salvador states that the promotion of a Government Commissioner (of the Judicial Section) was delayed for many years because he had concluded against the government in an important decision. "Un Grand Commissaire du gouvernement: Jean Romieu," *Conseil d'Etat, Livre jubilaire* (Paris, 1952), p. 331.
21. After two years service it is possible for an auditor, who in the opinion of the Vice-President and the Section Presidents does not measure up to the standard required, to be transferred outside the Conseil to an administrative post, but this, in fact, never occurs.
22. The retirement age for Maîtres des Requêtes is lower, but no Maître des Requêtes ever reaches retirement age in that rank.
23. In the Fourth Republic the Superior Council of the Magistrature was established to prevent abuses relative to advancement in the judiciary.
24. The judicial year runs from August 1 to July 31.
25. This figure is cited by Cassin in his "Introduction," but the figure is given in the statistical part of the same issue as 5,140. *Conseil d'Etat, Etudes et documents*, No. 2 (Paris, 1948), p. 89.
26. Cassin, "Introduction," *ibid.*, p. 12.

27. *Ibid.*, p. 13.   28. *Ibid.*
29. *JO, Débats parlementaires, Assemblée Nationale*, 14 mars 1953, p. 1893. Speech of the *rapporteur*, M. Joseph Wasmer.
30. *JO, Débats parlementaires, Assemblée Nationale*, 1953, pp. 1893–1905, 2362–80, and 1757–63.
31. *JO, Lois et décrets*, 1er octobre 1953, pp. 9593–94. Décrets no. 53–934 and 53–935, completed by décret no. 53–936 with *règlement d'administration publique*.
32. Décret no. 53–934, article 1.   33. *Ibid.*, article 2.
34. Décret no. 53–935, article 3.
35. Unfortunately a large number of these cases fell within the jurisdiction of the Administrative Tribunal of Paris, which was already overworked. For the Paris area the reform of 1953 merely had the effect of transferring the bottleneck from the Conseil d'Etat to the Administrative Tribunal.
36. Georges Cahen-Salvador, "De quelques personnalités qui ont illustré le Conseil d'Etat au XXe siècle," *Conseil d'Etat, Livre jubilaire*, pp. 377–78.
37. *Ibid.*, p. 380.   38. *Ibid.*
39. Gaston Jèze, "Collaboration du Conseil d'Etat et de la doctrine dans l'élaboration du droit administratif français," *ibid.*, p. 347.
40. Cahen-Salvador, "De quelques personnalités qui ont illustré le Conseil d'Etat," *ibid.*, p. 378.
41. *Ibid.*, p. 381.
42. C. J. Hamson, "Rule of Law in France," *The Times* (London), February 21, 1951, p. 5.
43. Henry Puget, "Tradition et progrès au sein du Conseil d'Etat," *Conseil d'Etat, Livre jubilaire*, p. 113.
44. Marcel Oudinot, "Le Rôle du rapporteur devant les formations administratives du Conseil d'Etat," *ibid.*, pp. 403–14.
45. They were called *Commissaires du Roi* during the July Monarchy.
46. Ordonnance du 2 février 1831.
47. Tony Sauvel, "Les Origines des Commissaires du Gouvernement auprès du Conseil d'Etat statuant au contentieux," *Revue du droit public*, LXV (1949), 14. The preamble of the ordinance stated: "Considerant qu'au moment où les parties obtiennent les avantages de la publicité et de la discussion orale il est convenable que l'administration et l'ordre public trouvent des moyens de défense analogues à ceux qui leur sont assurés devant les tribunaux ordinaires."
48. *Ibid.* According to Sauvel, the independence of the early Gov-

ernment Commissioners was appreciable. However, this view has been contested by Raymond Guillien, "Les Commissaires du Gouvernement près les juridictions administratives et, spécialement le Conseil d'Etat français," *Revue du droit public*, LXXI (1955), 283 and 303.

49. When he attends the meeting of the subsection where the report is discussed, the Government Commissioner may take part in the discussion. During the period when the subsection recesses for afternoon tea, the cases under consideration are often discussed, which has led to a saying that "la jurisprudence se fait à la buvette."

50. Gilbert Dauphin, *L'Administration consultative centrale* (Paris, 1932), pp. 66–67.

51. The total period thus became twelve years. *Conseil d'Etat, Etudes et documents*, No. 6 (Paris, 1952), p. 99. However, in 1954 the total period was increased to fifteen years for certain important positions where the appointment is made by the government (décret du 15 mai 1954).

52. London, 1942.

53. *Ibid.*, p. 17. Some of the duties which a cabinet chief may perform are described in the following note.

54. *Ibid.*, pp. 29–30. Some of the duties which Tissier performed while cabinet chief for Laval, and the list is by no means unusual, were (1) acting as Laval's personal secretary, (2) signing Laval's name on multitudes of papers, (3) passing out the secret funds of the Ministry of Interior, (4) preparing Laval's speeches, (5) briefing Laval during parliamentary debates, (6) correcting the proofs of the debate before they were published in the *Journal Officiel* so as to delete any inadvertent remarks the minister may have made in the heat of the debate, (7) buttonholing deputies in the corridor and asking them how they intended to vote and urging them to support the government.

4. THE LEGISLATIVE FUNCTION OF THE CONSEIL D'ETAT SINCE 1872

1. In 1947 bills introduced by members accounted for only a quarter of those passed. Half of those bills that became law were passed virtually unopposed. D. W. S. Lidderdale, *The Parliament of France* (London, 1951), pp. 178–79.

2. Loi du 24 mai 1872, article 8.

3. This period was not a full five years because the Conseil did not begin to function until August of 1872.

4. *Compte général des travaux du Conseil d'Etat depuis le 10 août 1872 jusqu'au 31 décembre 1877* (Paris, 1878), p. ix, hereafter cited as *Compte général*.
5. *Ibid.*, p. 7.
6. *Ibid.*, pp. 9–17.
7. *Compte général 1878–1882*, pp. vii–ix.
8. *Compte général 1883–1887*, pp. vi–vii.
9. *Compte général 1878–1882*, p. vii; *Compte général 1883–1887*, p. vi.
10. *Compte général 1872–1877*, p. viii.
11. Ernest Tarbouriech, "Du Conseil d'Etat comme organe législatif," *Revue du droit public*, 1894 (tome 2), p. 266, note 1.
12. Joseph Barthélemy and Paul Duez, *Traité élémentaire de droit constitutionnel* (Paris, 1926), p. 557.
13. Ricard, *JO, Documents parlementaires, Chambre des Députés*, 1891, annexe no. 1452, pp. 1348–58; Arnoux, *ibid.*, 1894, annexe no. 812, p. 1137; Marin, *ibid.*, 1920, annexe no. 222, pp. 105–8.
14. Barthélemy and Duez, *Traité élémentaire de droit constitutionnel*, p. 214; Waline, *Manuel élémentaire de droit administratif* (Paris, 1936), p. 67; Jacques Auboyer-Treuille, *L'Evolution des attributions législatives du Conseil d'Etat* (Paris, 1938), p. 233.
15. Joseph Barthélemy, *Essai sur le travail parlementaire* (Paris, 1934), p. 180.
16. After the law of April 7, 1902, a decree in the Conseil d'Etat was sufficient. This type of decree is discussed in Chapter V.
17. The law of December 18, 1940, did establish a Section on Legislation but, in spite of the name, this section, like the earlier Section on Legislation, dealt with exactly the same kind of matters as the other administrative sections.
18. *Conseil d'Etat, Assemblée Générale du 24 août 1940* (Royat, 1940), p. 5.
19. *Ibid.*, p. 7.
20. *Conseil d'Etat, Assemblée Générale du 19 août 1941* (Royat, 1941).
21. The text of the Pétain draft constitution was published by André Philip in the December 20, 1945, issue of *Le XXe siècle*. There is a possibility that this text is not the final draft. This text can also be found in L. Duguit, H. Monnier, and R. Bonnard, *Les Constitutions et les principales lois politiques de la France depuis 1789* (7éme éd., Paris, 1952), pp. 386 ff. The text is analyzed in Julien Laferrière, *Manuel de droit constitutionnel* (2ème éd., Paris, 1947), pp. 855 ff. Laferrière notes that Councilors of State established two drafts

NOTES TO 4: LEGISLATIVE FUNCTION OF THE CONSEIL 183

of the Constitution, one in 1941 and another in 1942, which they submitted to the Constitutional Committee of the National Council (p. 855).
22. *Conseil d'Etat, Etudes et documents,* No. 1 (1947), p. 90.
23. *Ibid.*
24. See the tabulation at the end of Chapter 4. It has been suggested that the procedure of declaring a bill urgent has been abused. Henry Puget, "Tradition et progrès au sein du Conseil d'Etat," *Conseil d'Etat, Livre jubilaire* (Paris, 1952), p. 120.
25. *Conseil d'Etat, Etudes et documents,* No. 1 (1947), p. 85.
26. *Ibid.*, No. 3 (1949), p. 104.   27. *Ibid.*   28. *Ibid.*
29. *Ibid.*, No. 2 (1948), p. 88.   30. *Ibid.*, No. 5 (1951), p. 110.
31. Loi du 3 août 1926, articles 1–13, was the enabling act for the decree-laws of 1926.
32. It should be noted that Article 13 was materially the same as the provision contained in the Constitutional Laws of 1875. Article 1 of the Constitutional Law of February 25, 1875, states: "The legislative power is exercised by two assemblies: the Chamber of Deputies and the Senate."
33. On this view see: Roger Pinto, "La Loi du 17 août 1948," *Revue du droit public,* LXIV (1948), 538; Jacques Donnedieu de Vabres, "Décrets-Lois et pouvoir réglementaires d'après la loi du 17 août 1948," *Recueil Dalloz,* 1949, Chronique, pp. 5–8; André de Laubadère, "Des 'pleins pouvoirs' aux 'demi décrets-lois,'" *Recueil Dalloz,* 1952, Chronique, p. 39.
34. This view stems from the great constitutional writer, Raymond Carré de Malberg.
35. Marcel Waline, Julien Laferrière, and Georges Vedel. See de Laubadère, "Des 'pleins pouvoirs' aux 'demi décrets-lois,'" *Recueil Dalloz,* 1952, Chronique, p. 39 and note 12. René Chapus is of the opinion that Article 13 did prohibit the grants, but that these grants can be justified, even though they violated the Constitution, on the grounds of stringent public necessity. "La Loi d'habilitation du 11 juillet 1953 et la question des décret-lois," *Revue du droit public,* LXIX, (1953), 998–1002.
36. Marcel Waline, *Traité élémentaire de droit administratif* (6ème éd., Paris, 1951), p. 37; Georges Vedel, *Manuel élémentaire de droit constitutionnel* (Paris, 1949), p. 501.
37. *Conseil d'Etat, Etudes et documents,* No. 4 (1950), p. 106.
38. Pinto, "La loi du 17 août 1948," *Revue du droit public,* LXIV (1948), 518–20 and 527.

39. *JO, Débats parlementaires, Assemblée Nationale*, 9 août 1948, p. 5526, and 11 août 1948, p. 5661.

40. René Capitant, in discussing the article proposed by André Philip, declared that it was not specific enough to prohibit recourse to decree-laws. He described the article as being "un coup d'épée dans l'eau." Capitant, a competent jurist, recognized the limited scope of the article, but it appears that he allowed his fears to be quieted by Pierre Cot, as he did not renew his objections. The wording of the article proposed by the chairman, Philip, is slightly different from Article 13, but the substance is the same. Philip's proposed article read: "L'assemblée dispose seule du pouvoir législatif et elle ne peut le déléguer." *Séances de la Commission de la Constitution*, I, 102–3. See also Pinto, "La Loi du 17 août 1948," *Revue du droit public*, LXIV (1948), 538–40; Pinto, *Eléments de droit constitutionnel* (Lille, 1948), p. 433.

41. *JO, Débats parlementaires, Assemblée Nationale*, 9 août 1948, p. 5530. René Capitant: "Les décrets-lois que le Gouvernement nous demande le pouvoir de prendre sont, à mon avis, contraires à la volonté du constituant et à la lettre de l'article 13 de la Constitution."

42. Article 5 granted the power to effect fiscal reforms and take economy measures by decree until January 1, 1949.

43. The government had requested an extension of the permanent "delegation" of the law of August 17 to certain other matters, in conformity with the views of the Conseil d'Etat on legality. However, the Assembly ignored the government's request and granted the powers for a limited period of time (until December 31, 1953) and conferred them on the existing government only. This placed the Conseil d'Etat in an awkward position for in its advisory opinion of February 6, 1953 (see Appendix A), it had declared that such a grant, unless permanent, was unconstitutional.

44. *Conseil d'Etat, Etudes et documents*, 1947–58, Nos. 1–12.

45. For the eleven months preceding August 1, 1945.

46. The statistical year runs from August 1 to July 31. After November 2, 1945, with the meeting of the First Constituent Assembly, the Conseil examined bills instead of proposed ordinances.

47. This figure lacks those decrees examined by the Section of the Interior.

48. Includes decrees examined under the law of July 11, 1953.

49. Includes decrees issued under the laws of August 14, 1954, and April 2, 1955.

50. Includes henceforth decrees issued under the laws of March 16, 1956, June 23, 1956, and June 30, 1956.

51. The decrease in the number of bills is owing to the crisis during 1958 which culminated in the demise of the Fourth Republic.

52. Includes decrees issued under the laws of June 26, 1957, August 7, 1957, and December 13, 1957, as well as 36 *ordonnances* issued under the law of June 3, 1958.

5. THE ADMINISTRATIVE FUNCTION OF THE CONSEIL D'ETAT SINCE 1872

1. Rules analogous to the French regulations of public administration are called "delegated legislation" in Britain and the United States. However, since French jurists have generally rejected the theory of delegation in regard to these acts, they are properly to be considered as administrative acts.

2. Adhémar Esmein, "De la délégation du pouvoir législatif," *Revue politique et publique* (Paris, 1894).

3. See Chapter 6.

4. Paul Duez and Guy Debeyre, *Traité de droit administratif* (Paris, 1952), p. 513.

5. *Ibid.*

6. *Recueil des arrêts du Conseil d'Etat*, 8 août 1919, Labonne, p. 737.

7. The *Revue* ceased appearing in 1928.

8. *Revue générale d'administration*, 1ère partie (1895), pp. 53–55.

9. Duez and Debeyre, *Traité de droit administratif*, pp. 33–34.

10. Georges Cahen-Salvador, "De quelques personnalités qui ont illustré le Conseil d'Etat au XXe siècle," *Conseil d'Etat, Livre jubilaire* (Paris, 1952), p. 380.

11. Loi du 1er juillet 1901, article 13.

12. Charles Seignobos, *L'Evolution de la Troisième République* (Vol. VIII of *Histoire de la France contemporaine*, ed. E. Lavisse, Paris, 1921), p. 223. The position of the Waldeck-Rousseau government was also conciliatory. François Goguel, *La Politique des partis sous la IIIe République* (Paris, 1946), pp. 115–16.

13. Under the Combes government the power to authorize new establishments of authorized congregations by the Conseil was withdrawn. The government was determined to reject all authorizations for new establishments.

14. Loi du 2 janvier 1907.

15. Marcel Waline, "L'Action du Conseil d'Etat dans la vie française," *Conseil d'Etat, Livre jubilaire*, p. 132.

16. René Martin, "Le Rôle consultatif du Conseil d'Etat en matière économique," *ibid.*, p. 418.

17. *Ibid.*, p. 420.

18. Pierre Mimin, *Le Socialisme municipal devant le Conseil d'Etat* (Paris, 1911), pp. 28–32; *Revue générale d'administration*, 3ème partie (1894), pp. 435–38.

19. *Revue générale d'administration*, 1ère partie (1900), p. 434.

20. Duez and Debeyre, *Traité de droit administratif*, pp. 540–41; and Chapter 7 above.

21. Henry Puget, "Le Droit des Associations," *Le Musée social* (juillet-août, 1926), p. 195.

22. Martin, "Le Rôle consultatif du Conseil d'Etat en matière economique," *Conseil d'Etat, Livre jubilaire*, p. 410.

23. *Ibid.*, p. 415.

24. Bernard Jouvin, "Les Débuts d'une Assemblée locale d'Outre-Mer," *Conseil d'Etat, Etudes et documents*, No. 3 (1949), p. 126.

25. *Ibid.*

26. Jean Ravanel, "Le Conseil d'Etat et les Assemblées des Territoires d'Outre-Mer," *Conseil d'Etat, Etudes et documents*, No. 4 (1950), p. 51.

27. *Ibid.*, pp. 53, 56, and 62.

28. Armand Guillon, "Avis et notes du Conseil d'Etat concernant l'organisation des pouvoirs publics," *Conseil d'Etat, Etudes et documents*, No. 2 (1948), p. 47.

29. *Ibid.*, pp. 45–47.

30. Georges Michel and Louis Canet, "Le Conseil d'Etat et la codification," *Conseil d'Etat, Livre jubilaire*, p. 469.

6. THE JUDICIAL FUNCTION OF THE CONSEIL D'ETAT SINCE 1872: I

1. F. Olivier-Martin, *Histoire du droit français* (2ème éd., Paris, 1951), pp. 666–67, 548–50.

2. *Dalloz Petit Code Administratif* (Paris, 1934), I, 1.

3. For example, the décret du 16 fructidor an III and article 3, chapitre V of the Constitution du 3 septembre 1791.

4. L. Duguit, H. Monnier, and R. Bonnard, *Les Constitutions et les principales lois politiques de la France depuis 1789* (7ème éd., Paris, 1952), p. 116.

NOTES TO 6: JUDICIAL FUNCTION OF THE CONSEIL: I   187

5. Alexis de Tocqueville, *Démocratie en Amérique* (Vol. I of *Oeuvres complètes*, éd. par J. P. Meyer, Paris, 1951), Part 1, p. 106.
6. Albert V. Dicey, *The Law of the Constitution* (9th ed., London, 1950), p. 359.
7. Paul Duez et Guy Debeyre, *Traité de droit administratif* (Paris, 1952), pp. 238–40.
8. *Ibid.*, p. 239.
9. Marcel Waline, *Traité élémentaire de droit administratif* (6ème éd., Paris, 1951), pp. 58–59.
10. Article 1384 of the *Code Civil* states: "A person is responsible not only for the damage which he causes by his own act but also for that which is caused by the acts of persons for whom he must answer, or by the things that he has under his custody. . . . Masters and employees [are responsible] for damages caused by their servants and employees in connection with the duties for which they have been employed."
11. Marcel Waline, *Traité élémentaire de droit administratif*, p. 59; Duez and Debeyre, *Traité de droit administratif*, pp. 239–40.
12. *Recueil des arrêts du Conseil d'Etat*, 6 décembre 1855, *Rothschild*, p. 708.
13. For the *Blanco* decision, see below in this chapter.
14. Duez and Debeyre, *Traité de droit administratif*, pp. 486–89; Waline, *Traité élémentaire de droit administratif*, pp. 103–6.
15. Gabriel Dufour, *Traité de droit administratif appliqué* (Paris, 1856), V, 128, cited in Duez and Debeyre, *Traité de droit administratif*, p. 487, note 3.
16. *Recueil des arrêts du Conseil d'Etat, Biens de la Famille d'Orléans*, 18 juin 1852, p. 258.
17. *Ibid., Duc d'Aumale et Michel Lévy*, 9 mai 1867, p. 476.
18. Of the Constitution of the Year VIII.
19. *Recueil des arrêts du Conseil d'Etat*, 1er supp., *Blanco*, Tribunal des Conflits, 8 février 1873, p. 61; Sirey, *Recueil général des lois et arrêts* (2ème partie, 1873), pp. 153 ff., with the conclusions of the Government Commissioner, David.
20. It was recognized in the conclusions of the Government Commissioner that basing the authority competent to declare the state a debtor on the decree of September 26, 1793, constituted a misinterpretation of that decree.
21. Waline, *Traité élémentaire de droit administratif*, p. 60.
22. Edouard Laferrière, *Traité de la juridiction administrative* (Paris, 1887), I, 437.

23. *Ibid.*

24. For the decision, the conclusions of the Government Commissioner, and an interesting commentary on the case, see Maurice Hauriou, *La Jurisprudence administrative de 1892 à 1929* (Paris, 1929), II, 447–62. Hauriou's three volumes contain his commentaries as originally published in the Sirey *Recueil*.

25. *Ibid.*, p. 451.   26. *Ibid.*

27. *Ibid.*, I, 573–88, especially the conclusions of the Government Commissioner, G. Teissier.

28. *Ibid.*, p. 576.   29. *Ibid.*, pp. 588 ff.

30. Of the important legal writers only Henri Berthélemy continued to support the old theory. See his *Traité élémentaire de droit administratif* (8ème éd., Paris, 1916), pp. 40–44 and 79–83, especially the footnotes. He continued to maintain the theory in the last edition of his *Traité*, in 1933.

31. Not to be confused with acts of management (*actes de gestion*).

32. *Recueil des arrêts du Conseil d'Etat*, 1er supp., *Pelletier*, Tribunal des Conflits, 26 juillet 1873, pp. 117–30.

33. *Ibid.*

34. Sirey, *Recueil général des lois et arrêts* (2ème partie, 1878), *Laumonnier-Carriol*, pp. 93 ff.; Edouard Laferrière, *Traité de la juridiction administrative*, I, 594–97.

35. *Feutry*, Tribunal des Conflits, 1908. See Hauriou, *La Jurisprudence administrative*, I, 576.

36. This development is reviewed in Armin Uhler, *Review of Administrative Acts* (Ann Arbor, Mich., 1942), pp. 112–42. See also Duez et Debeyre, *Traité de droit administratif*, pp. 692–704.

37. See Hauriou, *La Jurisprudence administrative*, II, 424–41, for the decision, the conclusions of the Government Commissioner, Jagerschmidt, and a commentary by Hauriou.

38. Edouard Lafarrière, *Traité de la juridiction administrative*, I, 399–414. A critique of the theory of the minister-judge published two years before the *Cadot* decision.

39. Since the reform of 1953 many types of cases formerly taken directly to the Conseil d'Etat, as a result of the *Cadot* decision, must now be taken to the administrative tribunals.

40. Duez and Debeyre, *Traité de droit administratif*, pp. 949–58; Waline, *Traité élémentaire de droit administratif*, pp. 295–97.

41. Sirey, *Recueil général des lois et arrêts* (2ème partie, 1875), pp. 95 ff. The Conseil rejected the petition, but on legal grounds.

42. *Ibid.*, 3ème partie, 1881, pp. 81 ff.
43. *Ibid.*, 3ème partie, 1889, pp. 19 ff.
44. Edouard Laferrière, *Traité de la juridiction administrative*, II, 37.
45. Duez and Debeyre, *Traité de droit administratif*, pp. 487–96; Waline, *Traité élémentaire de droit administratif*, pp. 105–8.
46. The general bibliography for this section is: Duez and Debeyre, *Traité de droit administratif*, pp. 336–410; Waline, *Traité élémentaire de droit administratif*, pp. 113–48; Louis Imbert, *L'Evolution du recours pour excès de pouvoir 1872–1900* (Paris, 1952); Raphaël Alibert, *Le Contrôle juridictionnel de l'administration* (Paris, 1926).
47. More precisely, it is that part of the state's patrimony known in French law as the *domaine privé de l'Etat*.
48. Imbert, *L'Evolution du recours pour excès de pouvoir*, p. 41.
49. Hauriou, *La Jurisprudence administrative*, II, 227–38.
50. *Recueil des arrêts du Conseil d'Etat*, 1911, p. 105.
51. Duez and Debeyre, *Traité de droit administratif*, p. 354; Waline, *Traité élémentaire de droit administratif*, p. 120.
52. *Recueil des arrêts du Conseil d'Etat*, 1903, pp. 619–20.
53. Duez and Debeyre, *Traité de droit administratif*, pp. 359–60.
54. *Recueil des arrêts du Conseil d'Etat*, 1911, *Abbé Anselme*, 8 avril 1911, p. 464.
55. *Storch*, 1905. See Hauriou, *La Jurisprudence administrative*, II, 18–31.
56. *Syndicate des propriétaires du Quartier Croix-de-Seguey-Tivoli*, ibid.
57. *Recueil des arrêts du Conseil d'Etat*, 1912, pp. 353–54.
58. Hauriou, *La Jurisprudence administrative*, I, 16.
59. See Hauriou's commentary on the *Epoux de Sigelas* decision (1928), *ibid.*, III, 792–800.
60. *Recueil des arrêts du Conseil d'Etat*, 1933, p. 1226.
61. Some authors—Waline, Imbert, and Rolland—claim five.
62. Loi du 7–14 octobre 1790.
63. *Recueil des arrêts du Conseil d'Etat*, 1905, *Lespinasse*, p. 757.
64. Hauriou, *La Jurisprudence administrative*, II, 319 ff.
65. Alibert, *Le Contrôle juridictionnel de l'administration*, p. 40.
66. It is said that he is answerable only to his conscience. The Government Commissioner resembles in certain respects the *procureur général* of the civil courts. However, there are differences which make the role of the Government Commissioner unique. The Government Commissioner always speaks last, whereas in some cases the

procureur général does not. In certain cases the *procureur général* does not speak at all, or he may limit his observations to specific points of law. The Government Commissioner always deals with the whole case, and specifically declares how he thinks it ought to be decided. A member of the Conseil has described his role as follows: "Il expose toute l'affaire; il analyse et critique tous les moyens, il analyse et critique de même toutes les règles de jurisprudence susceptibles d'être invoquées; bien souvent il montre la marche suivie par cette jurisprudence, souligne les étapes déjà franchies par elle et laisse entrevoir certaines étapes à venir. Enfin il conclut à l'admission ou au rejet de la requête." Tony Sauvel, "Les Origines des Commissaires du Gouvernement auprès du Conseil d'Etat statuant au contentieux," *Revue du droit public*, LXV (1949), 5. The name Government Commissioner has become somewhat of a misnomer; it does not accurately describe the function any more. Some writers have suggested that a more accurate designation for them would be "Law Commissioners" (*Commissaires des Lois*).

67. See for example, the *Fabrègues* decisions of 1909 and 1910; Hauriou, *La Jurisprudence administrative*, II, 397–98.

68. *Ibid.*, commentary of Hauriou, 398–402; Duez and Debeyre, *Traité de droit administratif*, pp. 402–3; Waline, *Traité élémentaire de droit administratif*, p. 162.

69. There exists a procedure by which the Conseil can delay the execution of an act. This is by means of an injunction (*sursis*), but it is rarely used. In the last ten years, the Conseil has granted injunctions on two occasions only.

7. THE JUDICIAL FUNCTION OF THE CONSEIL D'ETAT SINCE 1872: II

1. The lawyers (*avocats au Conseil d'Etat et à la Cour de Cassation*) must be on the list of the sixty allowed to plead before the Conseil d'Etat and the Court of Cassation.

2. There is on exception. Since 1952, the services of a lawyer are required for petitions in cassation.

3. The *déchéance quadriennale*, a statute of limitation that extinguishes claims against the public authorities after four years, makes the time limit of thirty years somewhat illusory. Before 1935 the *déchéance* period was five years.

4. The general bibliography for this section is: Edouard Laferrière, *Traité de la juridiction administrative* (Paris, 1887), I, 564–68, and II (1888), 115–360; Henri Berthélemy, *Traité élémentaire de*

droit administratif (8ème éd., Paris, 1916), pp. 76–86; Marcel Waline, *Traité élémentaire de droit administratif* (6ème éd., Paris, 1951), pp. 557–609; Paul Duez and Guy Debeyre, *Traité de droit administratif* (Paris, 1952), pp. 411–75 and 895–912; Paul Duez, *La Responsibilité de la puissance publique* (2ème éd., Paris, 1938); and Léon Duguit, *Les Transformations du droit public* (Paris, 1913), trans. by Harold and Frida Laski as *Law in the Modern State* (New York, 1919), pp. 197–242.

5. The classification of the action for damages under the law of public liability at the beginning of the Third Republic is taken from the first edition of Edouard Laferrière's *Traité*, published in 1887–88. Laferrière's was the first systematic treatise on administrative law.

6. Edouard Laferrière, *Traité de la juridiction administrative*, II, 174–76. For an explanation of acts of authority and acts of management, see Chapter 6 above.

7. In Chapter 6.

8. *De Fonscolombe* decision, Tribunal des Conflits, 11 avril 1908. Maurice Hauriou, *La Jurisprudence administrative* (Paris, 1929), I, 589 ff., with a commentary by Hauriou.

9. Hauriou, *La Jurisprudence administrative*, I, 515–16.

10. *Ibid.*, pp. 516–29. 11. *Ibid.*, p. 529. 12. *Ibid.*, pp. 529–39.
13. *Ibid.*, p. 529. 14. *Ibid.*, pp. 529–39. 15. *Ibid.*, III, 380 ff.

16. *Recueil des arrêts du Conseil d'Etat*, 1919, pp. 650–51.

17. Hauriou, *La Jurisprudence administrative*, I, 676 ff.

18. *Ibid.*, pp. 686 ff. 19. *Ibid.*, p. 686.

20. *Recueil des arrêts du Conseil d'Etat*, 1920, pp. 532–33.

21. Hauriou, *La Jurisprudence administrative*, I, 510 ff.

22. Another interesting example of the application of the theory of risk is the *Couitéas* decision (1923), *ibid.*, 698 ff.

23. Duez and Debeyre, *Traité de droit administratif*, pp. 440–41.

24. *Recueil des arrêts du Conseil d'Etat*, 1949, *Lecomte* decision, pp. 307–8.

25. Hauriou, *La Jurisprudence administrative*, I, 627–35.

26. *Ibid.*, pp. 636–54, with the conclusions of the Government Commissioner, Blum. Hauriou's commentary is adversely critical of the decision.

27. *Ibid.*, p. 643.

28. *Recueil des arrêts du Conseil d'Etat*, 1949, *Demoiselle Mimeur, Defaux et Besthelsemer* decisions, pp. 492–93.

29. Hauriou, *La Jurisprudence administrative*, III, 679–89, with the conclusions of the Government Commissioner, Georges Pichat.

30. *Ibid.*, pp. 679–80.
31. *Ibid.*, pp. 578–614, with the conclusions of the Government Commissioner, Chardenet.
32. Duez and Debeyre, *Traité de droit administratif*, p. 576.
33. *Ibid.*, p. 412, note 3.
34. Décret-loi du 6 septembre 1926 and décret-loi du 3 mai 1934.
35. Hauriou, *La Jurisprudence administrative*, III, 154–74, with the conclusions of the Government Commissioner, Tardieu.
36. *Ibid.*, p. 174.   37. *Ibid.*, pp. 154–67.   38. *Ibid.*, p. 174.
39. *Ibid.*, *Tichit* decision, 1912, pp. 175–81. In his commentary on this decision Hauriou explains more fully his views on judicial review.
40. Pascal Arrighi, "Hauriou: Un Commentateur des arrêts du Conseil d'Etat," *Conseil d'Etat, Livre jubilaire* (Paris, 1952), p. 344.
41. Hauriou, *La Jurisprudence administrative*, I, 78–84.
42. *Ibid.*, pp. 80–81. In Hauriou's words: "This omission of validation placed the Conseil d'Etat in an embarrassing position, because, during the course of the war the opinion was established that the decrees of *pleins pouvoirs* infringing on legislative matters must, to be valid, . . . have been foreseen and authorized by the legislator, or have been validated by a law afterwards."
43. Article 3 defined the powers of the President. The relevant parts of the article are: "He exercises surveillance and insures the execution [of the laws]. . . . He disposes of the armed forces. He nominates to all civil and military posts. . . ." L. Duguit, H. Monnier, and R. Bonnard, *Les Constitutions et les principales lois politiques de la France depuis 1789* (7ème éd., Paris, 1952), p. 291.
44. Hauriou, *La Jurisprudence administrative*, I, 78.
45. *Recueil des arrêts du Conseil d'Etat*, 1950, p. 426.
46. Duguit, Monnier, and Bonnard, *Les Constitutions de la France*, p. 554.
47. *Recueil des arrêts du Conseil d'Etat*, 1950, p. 426.
48. In his commentary on the *Dehaene* decision, Waline affirmed that it violated the Constitution. In his opinion only a parliamentary enactment could limit the right of civil servants to strike. *Revue du droit public* LXVI (1950), 691 ff.
49. Constitutional writers are unanimous in recognizing that the concrete dispositions of the Preamble have the force of positive law, unless an act of parliament has intervened. Thus, for the parliament, the value of the Preamble is "purely moral or political—a counsel given to the legislative authority." *Ibid.*, pp. 695–96.

50. Hauriou, *La Jurisprudence administrative*, I, 307–18, with the conclusions of the Government Commissioner.

51. Max Querrien, "Du droit jurisprudentiel au droit écrit: La Part du Conseil d'Etat dans l'élaboration du Statut de la Fonction Publique," *Conseil d'Etat, Livre jubilaire*, pp. 311–22.

52. *Recueil des arrêts du Conseil d'Etat*, 1895, p. 57.

53. André Soulier, *L'Instabilité ministérielle sous la Troisième République (1871–1938)* (Paris, 1939), pp. 130, 352.

54. Barthou stated in his letter of resignation: "The decisions of the Conseil d'Etat have not modified my opinion and it would be impossible for me, as Minister of Public Works, in negotiations with the companies of Orléans and of the Midi, to draw inspiration from a decision before which I bow, but which my preceding attitude does not permit me to apply." *Ibid.*, p. 352, note 52.

55. *Fédération nationale non syndiquée des professeurs* decision, *Recueil des arrêts du Conseil d'Etat*, 1935, p. 327.

56. Disregarding the associations of civil servants set up under the Vichy government by the law of September 14, 1941.

57. Hauriou, *La Jurisprudence administraitve*, II, 227–38; Pierre Mimin, *Le Socialisme municipal devant le Conseil d'Etat* (Paris, 1951), pp. 54–57.

58. *Recueil des arrêts du Conseil d'Etat*, 1896, pp. 642–43.

59. Hauriou, *La Jurisprudence administrative*, I, 144–68, with the conclusions of the Government Commissioner, Romieu. Hauriou is not completely in accord with the decision; see Mimin, *Le Socialisme municipal devant le Conseil d'Etat*, pp. 47–53.

60. Cited from Duez and Debeyre, *Traité de droit administratif*, p. 541.

61. *Ibid.*, pp. 541–42.

62. For example, the *Ville de Paris* decision, Hauriou, *La Jurisprudence administrative*, III, 427–31.

63. Waline, "L'Action du Conseil d'Etat dans la vie française," *Conseil d'Etat, Livre jubilaire*, pp. 131–40.

64. M. Letourneur, "Les 'Principes généraux du Droit' dans la jurisprudence du Conseil d'Etat," *Conseil d'Etat, Etudes et documents*, No. 5 (1951), p. 29.

65. *Ibid.*, p. 31.

66. Sirey, *Recueil général des lois et arrêts* (3ème partie, 1945), pp. 14 ff., with the conclusions of the Government Commissioner, Chenot.

67. Tony Bouffandeau, "Le Juge de l'excès de pouvoir jusqu'à la

Libération," *Conseil d'Etat, Etudes et documents,* No. 1 (1947), pp. 24–26.

68. Waline, "L'Action du Conseil d'Etat dans la vie française," *Conseil d'Etat, Livre jubilaire,* p. 136; R. Odent, "Conclusions sur l'épuration administrative," *Conseil d'Etat, Etudes et documents,* No. 1 (1947), pp. 48–68.

69. M. Letourneur, "Les 'Principles généraux du droit' dans la jurisprudence du Conseil d'Etat," *Conseil d'Etat, Etudes et documents,* No. 5 (1951), pp. 26–27.

70. *Ibid.,* p. 31. 71. *Ibid.*

BIBLIOGRAPHY

Alibert, Raphaël. Le Contrôle juridictionnel de l'administration. Paris, Payot, 1926.
Auboyer-Treuille, Jacques. L'Evolution des attributions législatives du Conseil d'Etat. Paris, Rodstein, 1938.
Aucoc, Léon. Le Conseil d'Etat avant et depuis 1789. Paris, Imprimerie nationale, 1876.
Barthélemy, Joseph. Essai sur le travail parlementaire. Paris, Delagrave, 1934.
Barthélemy, Joseph, and Duez, Paul. Traité de droit constitutionnel. Nouv. éd. Paris, Dalloz, 1933.
—— Traité élémentaire de droit constitutionnel. Paris, Dalloz, 1926.
Béquet, Léon. Le Conseil d'Etat, Organisation-fonctionnement. Paris, DuPont, 1891.
Berthélemy, Henri. Traité élémentaire de droit administratif. 8ème éd. Paris, Rousseau, 1916.
Bonnard, R. See Duguit, Léon, H. Monnier, and R. Bonnard.
Braibant, G. See Long, M.
[Broglie, duc Léonce-Victor de] "Des Tribunaux administratifs," Revue française (novembre, 1928), pp. 58–132.
Chardon, Henri. L'Administration de la France. Paris, Perrin, 1908.
Code, administratif (Petite collection Dalloz). 2 vols. Paris, Dalloz, 1934.
Code administratif (Petits codes Dalloz), 2ème éd. Paris, Dalloz, 1951.
Compte général des travaux du Conseil d'Etat depuis le 10 août 1872 jusqu'au 31 décembre 1877. Paris, Imprimerie nationale, 1878.
Compte général des travaux du Conseil d'Etat depuis le 1er janvier 1878 jusqu'au 31 décembre 1882. Paris, Imprimerie nationale, 1888.
Compte général des travaux in Conseil d'Etat depuis le 1er janvier 1883 jusqu'au 31 décembre 1887. Paris, Imprimerie nationale, 1890.
Conseil d'Etat, Etudes et documents. Nos. 1–12 (1947–58). Paris, Imprimerie nationale.

Conseil d'Etat, Livre jubilaire publié pour commémorer son cent cinquantième anniversaire. Paris, Sirey, 1952.
Dauphin, Gilbert. L'Administration consultative centrale. Paris, Rivière, 1932.
Debeyre, Guy. *See* Duez, Paul, and Guy Debeyre.
Dicey, Albert Venn. Introduction to the Study of the Law of the Constitution. 9th Ed., by E. S. C. Wade. London, Macmillan, 1939.
Dreyfus, Robert. De M. Thiers à Marcel Proust. Paris, Plon, 1939.
—— *See* Halévy, Daniel.
Duez, Paul. Le Responsibilité de la puissance publique. 2ème éd. Paris, Sirey, 1938.
—— Les Actes de gouvernement. Paris, Sirey, 1935.
—— and Debeyre, Guy. Traité de droit administratif. Paris, Dalloz, 1952.
—— *See* Barthélemy, Joseph.
Duguit, Léon. Les Transformations du droit public. Paris, Colin, 1913. Trans. as *Law in the Modern State*, by Harold and Frida Laski. New York, Huebsch, 1919.
—— H. Monnier and R. Bonnard. Les Constitutiones et les principales lois politiques de la France depuis 1789. 7ème éd., par Georges Berlia. Paris, Librarie général de droit et de jurisprudence, 1952.
Esmein, Adhémar. Eléments de droit constitutionnel français et comparé. 5ème éd. Paris, Larose, 1909. 8ème éd. revue par Henry Nézard, 2 vols. Paris, Sirey, 1927–28.
Ferrat, André. La République à réfaire. Paris, Gallimard, 1945.
Garner, John W. "Judicial Control of Administrative and Legislative Acts in France," *American Poltiical Science Review*, IX (1915), 637–65.
Goldenberg, Léo. Le Conseil d'Etat, juge du fait. Paris, Dalloz, 1932.
Guillien, Raymond. "Les Commissaires du gouvernement près les juridictions administratives et, spécialement près le Conseil d'Etat français," *Revue de droit public*, LXXI (1955), 281–303.
Guillois, A. "L'Organisation de la juridiction administrative: projets de réforme," *Revue du droit public*, XL (1923), 84–99.
Halévy, Daniel, and Dreyfus, Robert. "Un débat sur 'le choix des Conseillers d'Etat, 1872–1875,'" *Bulletin de la Société d'histoire moderne*, 1936, Nos. 10 et 11.
Hamson, C. J. Executive Discretion and Judicial Control, an Aspect of the French Conseil d'Etat. London, Stevens, 1954.
Hauriou, Maurice. De la formation de droit administratif français depuis l'an VIII. Paris, Berger-Levrault, 1893.

—— La Jurisprudence administrative de 1892 à 1929. 3 vols. Paris, Sirey, 1929.

Imbert, Louis. L'Evolution du recours pour excès de pouvoir 1872–1900. Paris, Dalloz, 1952.

Jèze, Gaston. "Lenteurs de la procédure devant le Conseil d'Etat," *Revue du droit public*, XXXIII (1916), 65–66.

Laferrière, Edouard. Traité de la juridiction administrative. 2 vols. Paris, Berger-Levrault, 1887–88. 2ème éd., 1896.

Laferrière, Julien. Manuel de droit constitutionnel. 2ème éd. Paris, Domat Montchrestien, 1947.

—— "L'Organisation de la juridiction administrative, Réformes et projets de réforme," *Revue du droit public*, XXXVII (1920), 553–73; XXXVIII (1921), 109–63.

Laubadère, André de. Traité élémentaire de droit administratif. Paris, Librarie générale de droit et de jurisprudence, 1953.

Letourneur, M., and Méric, J. Conseil d'Etat et juridictions administratives. Paris, Colin, 1955.

Long, M., P. Weil, and G. Braibant. Les Grands Arrêts de la jurisprudence administrative. Paris, Sirey, 1956.

Mélanges Maurice Hauriou. Paris, Sirey, 1929.

Mimin, Pierre. Le Socialisme municipal devant le Conseil d'Etat. Paris, Sirey, 1911.

Monnier, H. *See* Duguit, Léon, H. Monnier, and R. Bonnard.

Oliver-Martin, François. Histoire du droit français. 2ème éd. Paris, Domat Montchrestien, 1951.

Puget, Henry. "Le Droit des associations," *Le Musée sociale*, juillet-août 1926, pp. 193–250.

Rapport au Garde des sceaux, présenté au nom de la Commission d'études pour la réforme du Conseil d'Etat, par M. Henry Puget. Paris, 1945. (Typewritten, 51 pp.)

Recueil des arrêts du Conseil d'Etat et des décisions du Tribunal des Conflits. Paris, 1821–.

Recueil des lois et règlements concernant le Conseil d'Etat. Paris, Imprimerie nationale, 1932.

Revue du droit public et de la science politique, 1894–.

Rolland, Louis. "La Réaction contre les abus du favoritisme," *Revue du Droit Public*, XXVII (1911), 571–600.

Sauvel, Tony. "Les Origines des commissaires du gouvernement auprès du Conseil d'Etat statuant au contentieux," *Revue du droit public*, LXV (1949), 5–20.

Schwartz, Bernard. French Administrative Law and the Common Law World. New York, New York University Press, 1954.
Sieghart, Marguerite A. Government by Decree. London, Stevens, 1950.
Sirey, publisher. Recueil général des lois et arrêts. 1791–.
Street, Harry. Governmental Liability. Cambridge, Cambridge University Press, 1953.
Tissier, Pierre. I Worked with Laval. London, Harrap, 1942.
Uhler, Armin. Review of Administrative Acts. Ann Arbor, Mich., University of Michigan Press, 1942.
Varagnac. "Le Conseil d'Etat," *Revue de deux mondes*, CXII (1892), 771–810; CXIII (1892), 288–318.
Waline, Marcel. Traité élémentaire de droit administratif. 6ème éd. Paris, Sirey, 1951.
Weil, Prosper. Les Conséquences de l'annulation d'un acte administratif pour excès de pouvoir. Paris, Pedone, 1952.
—— *See* Long, M.

TABLE OF CASES

The designation TC following a case means it was heard by the Tribunal of Conflicts.

Ambrosini (1912)	147
Anguet (1911)	148
Aumale, duc d', et Michel Lévy (1867)	117, 126
Aumale, duc d', et Prince Murat (1887)	126
Auxerre (1905)	145
Blanco (1873, TC)	118–19, 124, 142
Bonnardot (1896)	160–61
Boulangers de Poitiers (1901)	160–61
Brunet (1919)	145–46
Cadot (1889)	13, 125–26, 164
Cames (1895)	146
Carville (1896)	135
Casanova (1901)	129, 160
Chabot (1903)	129
Colas (1920)	147
Compagnie du gaz de Bordeau (1916)	152–53
Compagnies de Chemin de Fer de l'Est (1907)	132
Compagnies de Chemin de Fer de P.-O. et Midi (1895)	159
Couitéas (1923)	191 (n. 22)
Dehaene (1950)	158, 192 (n. 48)
Dordogne, Département de la (1907)	145
Feutry (1908, TC)	121–22, 124, 143
Fonscolombe, de (1908, TC)	122–24, 143
Greco (1905)	145
Heyriès (1918)	156–57
Lafage (1912)	131
Laumonnier-Carriol (1877, TC)	123
Lemonnier (1918)	148–49
Lepreux (1899)	143–45

Lespinasse (1905)	135
Marquigny (1880, TC)	126
Maurel (1933)	132
Mogambury (1892)	158–59
Napoléon Bonaparte, Prince (1875)	126
Orléans, Biens de Famille d' (1852)	116–17, 126
Paris, Ville de (1895)	161–62
Pelletier (1873, TC)	123–24
Regnault-Desroziers (1919)	146–47
Richemond (1911)	129
Rothschild (1855)	116
Syndicat des propriétaires du Croix-de-Sequey-Tivoli (1906)	130
Terrier (1903)	120–21, 143
Thérond (1910)	151–52
Trompier-Gravier (1944)	163
Winkell et Rosier (1909)	154–55

INDEX

Acts, of authority, 115–16, abandonment of, 119–22, governmental liability for, 142–44; of management, 115–16, abandonment of, 119–22, governmental liability for, 142–44; of state, 116–17, 126–27

Administrative Tribunals, 128, 141, 151, 165; establishment of, 61–62; of Paris, 180(n. 35); *see also* Councils of Prefecture

Alibert, Raphaël, 80

Alsace-Lorraine, 103

Andral (Vice-President of the Conseil d'Etat), 80

Associations, legal recognition of, 107

Aucoc, Léon, 12

Auditors, 64–66, 179(n. 21); origins of, 10; recruitment of, 28–30, 52–54, 173(n. 5); number, function and promotion of, 36–40, 52, 57–58, 178(n. 64*tab.*)

Audren de Kerdrel (deputy), 35; quoted, 25

Bardoux, Benjamin, 24
Barrot, Odilon, 34
Barthélemy, Joseph, 81
Barthou, Louis, 43, 159, 193(n. 54)
Batbie, Anselme, 12, 19, 23, 25, 35; quoted, 22, 26
Bertauld, Charles, 24

Bills, of general interest, 75–78; of local interest, 75–78; role of the Conseil d'Etat in drafting, 78–79; advisory role of the Conseil on, 79–80, 81, 82–84; examined by the Conseil 1944–58, 90 (*tab.*); introduced by members of legislature, 181(n. 1)

Blum, Léon, 68, 69, 179(n. 17); quoted, 149

Bourse, 107

Briand, Aristide, 78, 122, 177(n. 53)

Broglie, Duc Albert de, 19, 20, 26, 175–76(n. 31)

Broglie, Duc Léonce Victor de, 14

Cahen-Salvador, Georges, 65, 179 (n. 20)

Capitant, René, 88; quoted, 184 (nn. 40, 41)

Casimir-Périer, Jean Paul Pierre, 159

Cassin, René, 47, 48, 59, 60

Chasseloup-Laubat, Marquis de, 19, 21

Civil servants, right to strike, 155–58; right to form unions, 160

Civil service, 3–4

Code Civil, 1, 110, 116, 118, 142

Colrat, Maurice, 43

Conseil d'Etat, dual role of, 1; origin of, 2; technical counselor of the government, 6–11; Provisional Commission (1870–72), 15–16; Vice-President, 21, 27–28, 47, 52, 55, 57–58, 62–64; organization in 1872, 27–34; judicial section, 31–32, 39–40, 55–56, 92, 111–67, 171, 179(n. 19); administrative sections, 31–32, 54–55, 182(n. 17); General Assembly, 31–32, 55; Public Assembly, 31–32, 56; legislative function, 32–33, 72–91; removal of members, 35–36, 47–48; detached-service activities of members, 37–38, 70–71, 181(n. 51); overloaded docket, 40–44, 59–62, 139; under Vichy, 45–46, 80–81; Permanent Commission, 47, 49, 54, 82–84; reform of, 48–52; government commissioners (administrative sections), 50; Plenary Assembly, 56; independence of, 58–59; role of reporter on, 66–67; internal procedure, 66–68, 136–37; government commissioner (judicial section), 67–68, 137, 177(n. 46), 180–82(nn. 47–49), 189–90(n. 66); administrative function, 92–110; lawyers practicing before, 130, 136, 141, 190(n. 1); and constitutionality of laws, 154–56; and suspension of a law, 156

Conseil du roi, 2, 111

Constitution, of the Year VIII, 1, 5, 94, 112, 122–23; Vichy draft, 81, 182–83(n. 21); of 1946, 93, 160, article 13, 85–86, 169–70, 183(n. 35), 184(n. 40), preamble, 157–58; of 1958, 90, 93, 109

Consultative councils and commissions, 3, 69–70, 110

Contracts, administrative, *see* Damages, action for, under the law of public liability

Coulon, Georges, 63, 103

Councilors of State, 10–11, 39–40, 66; origins of, 2; appointment of, 24–27, 34–35, 57–58, 176(n. 42); in special service, 30–31, 49–50; number of, 52, 178(n. 64*tab*.)

Councils of Prefecture, 23, 50, 165; reform of, 41–44, 60–61; jurisdiction of, 127–28, 141, 151, 153–54; *see also* Administrative Tribunals

Court, of Accounts, 4, 53, 138, 179(n. 16); administrative, 5–6; of Cassation, 5, 18, 20, 27; *see also* Administrative tribunals, Tribunal of Conflicts

Crédit foncier, 107

Damages, action for, under the law of public liability, 127; compared with plea of *ultra vires*, 140–41; and governmental liability, 142–50; and administrative contracts, 150–53; and theory of unforeseen circumstances, 152–53

David (government commissioner), 126; quoted, 118–19

Debré, Michel, 69

Declaration of the Rights of Man (1789), 163, 170

Déclinatoire de compétence, 117

Decree-laws, 3, 84–90; *see also* Laws

Decrees, 8, 95–97
   September 26, 1793 (authority competent to declare the state a debtor), 116, 119, 187 (n. 20)
   September 15, 1870 (suspending the Conseil d'Etat), 15

September 19, 1870 (abrogating Article 75 of the Constitution of the Year VIII), 118
August 10, 1899 (regulating working conditions under government contracts), 162
September 10, 1914 (suspending Article 65 of the law of April 22, 1905), 157
Deligne, Maurice, 71
Dicey, Albert V., ix, 174(nn. 17, 19); views on French administrative law, 11–15
Doctrine, as source of administrative law, 114–15
Dreyfus, Robert, 176(n. 52)
Ducrocq, Théophile, 12
Dufaure, Jean, 16, 18, 22, 24, 26, 58, 118; quoted, 25
Duguit, Léon, 130
Dupuy, Charles, 159
Duval, Raoul, 34

Ecole libre des sciences politiques, 50–51, 53
Ecole nationale d'administration, 51, 52–54, 57
Esmein, Adhémar, 94
Etudes et Documents (periodical), 59

Fault, "service-connected" and "personal," 123–24, 147–50
Faustin-Hélie (Vice-President of the Conseil d'Etat), 36
Free French Government, London National Committee, 46; Commission on Legislation, 46, 81; Judicial Commission, 46–47; Committee of National Liberation, 47, 52; Juridical Committee, 47, 81–82
French Community, 109–10
French Union, 108–9
Freycinet Plan, 105

Gambetta, Léon, 24, 33; quoted, 22
Gaslonde, Charles, 34
Gaulle, General Charles de, 45
Grévy, Jules, 35
Grunebaum-Ballin (Maître des Requêtes), 78

Halévy, Daniel, 176(n. 42)
Hauriou, Maurice, 144–45, 154–56; quoted, 144, 155, 192(n. 42)

Injunction, 190(n. 69)
Inspection of Finance, 4, 53, 179 (n. 16)
Institut d'études politiques, 53

Jèze, Gaston, 64
Journal Officiel (periodical), 99

Ladmirault, General de, 124
Laferrière, Edouard, 12–13, 53–64, 119, 123, 126–27, 191(n. 5); quoted, 127
Laferrière, Julien, quoted, 41–42
Laval, Pierre, 71, 181(n. 54)
Law, 9; administrative, 11, 14, 114; and the legislatives process, 72; general principles of, 162–64
Laws:
August 16–24, 1790 (judicial organization), 4, 111–12
July 19, 1845 (organization of the Conseil d'Etat), 17
March 8, 1849 (organization of the Conseil d'Etat), 17–18
May 24, 1872 (organization of the Conseil d'Etat), 17, 94, 118, 127; elaboration of, 18–27; content of, 27–34; and legislative role of the Conseil d'Etat, 73–74
February 25, 1875 (organization of the public powers), 34–35, 157, 183(n. 32)

Laws (*Continued*):
July 13, 1879 (on the Conseil d'Etat), 36–37
April 5, 1884 (municipal organization), 98, 161
July 1, 1901 (on associations), 63, 80, 95, 102–3
April 22, 1905 (finance law), Article 65, 155–57
December 9, 1905 (separation of church and state), 9, 102–3
July 13, 1911 (finance law), 96
March 30, 1915 (retroactive validation of decrees), 157
September 9, 1919 (mining concessions), 104
May 3, 1921 (war damages), 147
September 6, 1926 (decree-law on Councils of Prefecture), 43
November 5, 1926 (decree-law on administrative decentralization), 164
December 28, 1926 (decree-law on municipal enterprise), 164
May 5, 1934 (decree-law on jurisdiction of Councils of Prefecture), 43–44
July 10, 1940 (delegation of powers to Marshal Pétain), 85
December 18, 1940 (organization of the Conseil d'Etat), 45, 80, 94, 182(n. 17)
July 31, 1945 (ordinance on organization of the Conseil d'Etat), 54, 82, 127; elaboration of, 48–52
October 19, 1946 (civil service), 159, 160
August 17, 1948 (grant of special powers), 86–88, 90, 108, 184(n. 43)
July 11, 1953 (grant of special powers), 61, 86, 89–90, 184(n. 43)

Lefèvre-Pontalis, Amédée, 23; quoted, 24
Lefèvre-Pontalis, Antonin, 21, 23
Legislation, delegated, 8, 166, 173 (n. 11), 185(n. 1)
Letourneur, Maxim, quoted, 164
Liability, governmental, *see* Damages, action for, under the law of public liability
Limpérani, François, 29

MacMahon, Marshal Marie E. P. de, 35, 58
Maginot, André, 65, 69
Maîtres des Requêtes, 10, 66, 179 (n. 22); origins of, 2; number and appointment of, 28, 36, 39–40, 52, 57–58, 178(n. 64*tab*.)
Marie, André, 88
Marin, Louis, 42–43, 49
Mayer, René, 61, 69, 71
Minister-judge, doctrine of, 125–26, 127–28
Montesquieu, Charles Louis de Secondat, Baron de Brède et de, 4, 24, 111
Municipal enterprise, 79; attitude of the Conseil d'Etat toward, 105–6, 160–61

Nail, Louis, 42
Napoleon I, 1
Napoleon III, 7, 117
National Economic Council, 70

Palais Royal, 64
Papal acts, 102; *Vehementer*, 103
Parlements, 111
Pétain, Marshal Philippe, 45, 81, 85, 178(n. 2)
Petition, for appreciation of validity, 138; in cassation, 138
Philip, André, 184(n. 40)

Picard, Alfred, 65, 70
Plea of *ultra vires*, 9, 14, 61, 166; admissibility, 128–32, 136; cost, 131; parallel remedy, 131; grounds of annulment, 133–36; form of decision, 137; consequences of annulment, 137–38; compared with *pleine juridiction*, 140–41
Porché, Alfred, 47, 80, 178(n. 4)
Powers, separation of, 4, 111–12, 115–16
Public service, doctrine of, 119, 120–22, 165
Puget, Henry, 48

Raudot, Claude-Marie, 21, 33, 34; quoted, 22
Recours de l'excès de pouvoir, see Plea of *ultra vires*
Recours de pleine juridiction, 141–42, 153–54; see also Damages, action for, under the law of public liability
Regulation of public administration, 8–9, 72, 93–95, 131–32
Rémusat, Paul de, 19
Responsibility, see Damages, action for, under the law of public liability
Revue générale d'administration (periodical), 99
Reynal Convention, 159
Reynaud, Paul, 88

Rivet, Jacques, 23
Romieu, Jean, 68, 158; quoted, 120–21
Rousseau, Jean Jacques, 112

Saint-Marc-Girardin (deputy), 19
Statute of limitations, for creditors of the state, 190(n. 3)
Superior Council of the Magistrature, 179(n. 23)

Tardieu, André, 155
Target, Paul Louis, 23
Teissier, Georges, 68, 121; quoted, 122, 123–24
Thiers, Adolphe, 7, 16, 21, 24, 25, 26, 34, 35, 58, 175(n. 23); quoted, 175(n. 28)
Tissier, Pierre, 71, 181(n. 54)
Tocqueville, Alexis de, 2, 14; quoted, 113
Tribunal of Conflicts, 165; in Second Republic, 18; establishment in 1872, 20, 27, 118; jurisprudence of, 118–19, 121–23, 143

Ultra vires, see Plea of *ultra vires*

Villeneuve, Hébrard de, 70

Waline, Marcel, 192(n. 48); quoted, 192(n. 49)
Wallon, Henri, 34